AN

HISTORICAL ACCOUNT

OF

AMERICAN COINAGE.

BY JOHN H. HICKCOX,

MEMBER OF THE ALBANY INSTITUTE.

WITH PLATES.

ALBANY, N. Y.:

JOEL MUNSELL, 78 STATE STREET.

LONDON: TRÜBNER & CO.

1858.

Bowers and Merena Galleries, Inc.

Reprint 1988

Entered according to Act of Congress, in the year 1858,

BY JOHN H. HICKCOX,

In the Clerk's Office of the District Court for the Northern District
of New York.

ISBN 0-943161-07-X (pbk.)

Bowers and Merena Galleries, Inc.
Publications Department
Box 1224
Wolfeboro, NH 03894

Edition 200.   5 copies on large paper.

INSCRIBED

TO

MY FATHER.

PREFACE.

The design of this work is to give an account of the legally authorized coinage of the United States of America, during the periods of their colonial history and their existence as a united republic. Nothing as comprehensive has heretofore been attempted, nor is there any separate publication on either our colonial or early federal coinage. The materials have been collected by consulting early periodicals, congressional and legislative documents and other works, and through an extensive correspondence with gentlemen in other states.

In the concluding chapter is given a catalogue of pieces which have not been legally issued, and can not, with one or two exceptions, be considered as tradesmen's tokens, but are merely the inventions of individuals, sometimes proposed as specimens or patterns of coinage for the newly formed republic. As such they are interesting and very suggestive. Another division remains to be investigated—the history of our American tokens, and the author would be happy if he should find an opportunity to illustrate this portion also. The topic is not less interesting and far more extensive than that under review in the following pages.

The *modern* coinage of the United States having been quite fully exhibited in the valuable treatise by Messrs. Eckfeldt and Du Bois, it has not been deemed expedient to repeat the engravings contained in that work.

I desire in this public manner, to express my obligations to Mr. B. H. Hall, of Troy; Mr. C. J. Hoadley, State Librarian of Connecticut; Mr. C. I. Ihrie, State Librarian of New Jersey; Mr. G. F. Houghton, of St. Albans, Vt.; Mr. N. C. Rexford, and Mr. W. J. Howard, of New York; Mr. H. M. Brooks, of Salem, Mass.; Mr. J. Colburn, of Boston; Mr. Brantz Mayer, and S. F. Streeter, of Baltimore; Rev. Dr. Murray, Mr. L. Condict, and Francis B. Cheetwood, of Elizabeth, N. J.; Col. J. Ross Snowden, Director of the U. S. Mint; Mr. H. A. Homes and Dr. F. B. Hough, of Albany; S. H. Parsons, of Middletown, Conn.; Mr. S. Alofsen, of Jersey City; Mr. S. F. Haven, Librarian of the American Antiquarian Society, and Mr. N. Bouton, Cor. Secretary of the New Hampshire Historical Society.

NEW YORK STATE LIBRARY, Albany, July 12, 1858.

New Introduction

By Q. David Bowers, 1988

Among all substantive 19th-century publications dealing with the subject of American numismatics, *An Historical Account of American Coinage*, by John H. Hickcox, published in 1858, is one of the very rarest. Indeed, the copyright page of the volume from which this reprint is taken specifically notes that just 200 copies were produced, plus five others on large paper. How many copies have survived the sands of time since 1858 is not known, but the tome is sufficiently rare that in the course of buying and selling many collections and attendant numismatic libraries over a period of several decades, the present writer has encountered but two or three.

The copy from which this reprint was made was earlier owned by J. deLagerberg of Passaic, New Jersey, much later passing into the library of Nelson Thorson, a prominent figure in American numismatic circles in the 1930s. From there is went into the library of Charles M. Johnson, the noted Long Beach, California numismatic bibliophile, after which is was stocked by George Kolbe, the numismatic bookseller from whom it was acquired several years past.

When Hickcox's work was published it stood alone as the only available (if an edition of 200 can be considered "available") text detailing colonial, state, and other early United States issues. Up to that time precious little had been published in America on the subject of numismatics, with the only other large book, *A Manual of Gold and Silver Coins and Bullion*, by Eckfeldt and DuBois, 1842, being primarily devoted to world coins. As it turned out, the very next year, 1859, saw the appearance of *The American Numismatical Manual*, by Montroville Wilson Dickeson, which was more elaborate than the Hickcox work and which contained much more information. Perhaps because of Dickeson's opus, and its subsequent 1860 reprint, (retitled slightly as *The American Numismatic Manual*) Hickcox's pioneering work has never received the attention it deserves. Still, among bibliophiles it has been highly desired, as perhaps the price of $375 marked by George Kolbe on the large-paper version from which this reprint was taken, indicates.

It was not until 1875 that Sylvester S. Crosby's definitive *The Early Coins of America* appeared, which surely had as one of its foundation stones the Hickcox work.

While a later generation of numismatic writers could draw upon a vast corpus of earlier works, this option was not available to Hickcox. As the list of credits in his work reveals, he went to primary sources: the State Librarian of Connecticut, the Director of the United States Mint, and others who were keepers of original data.

At the same time he was cognizant of the numismatic hobby, not realizing that the several dozen serious collectors of United States coins who lived at that time would be the predecessors of millions of collectors yet to come. An early price guide was furnished, and can be found on the second leaf following page 147 of the present text. One wonders what Hickcox would have throught if he had known that the dollar of 1804, valued at $5, would be worth nearly one hundred thousand times that amount a century and a quarter later!

It is the hope of the reprinter that the present generation of numismatists will find *An Historical Account of American Coinage* to be an interesting addition to their numismatic libraries.

Q. David Bowers
April 15, 1988

CONTENTS.

CHAPTER I.

CHAPTER II.

CHAPTER III.

CHAPTER IV.

American Coinage.

CHAPTER I.

COINS OF THE COLONIAL PERIOD.

COINAGE OF MASSACHUSETTS.

When the first charter of the " Governor and Company of Massachusetts Bay in New England" was recalled in 1684, among the reasons assigned for that proceeding was in substance this; that the colonists had assumed under it, too many privileges. The commissioners of the king at a date anterior to this event, had presented a long list of objectionable laws and parts of laws "in the booke entitled the Booke of Generall Lawes and Libertjes concerning the Inhabitants of the Massachusetts," and among them was enumerated the law concerning the mint.

The mint of the colony was established, as will be hereafter shewn, in the year 1652,[1] and the fact that no notice had heretofore been taken of the

[1] Charles I was beheaded Jan. 30, 1648-9. Cromwell assumed his title Dec. 16, 1653.

practice of coining, argues either that Parliament was too much engaged in caring for domestic troubles, or else too much was presumed on the loyalty of the colonists. Both reasons probably enter into the explanation of the case, but that the charge of infringement was not considered a very grave one, would appear from the fact that it was tacitly allowed for more than twenty years after Charles II came to the throne; and during Sir Edmund Andros's administration when an application was made to continue it, the subject was referred to the mint master who, according to Hutchinson, reported against it merely upon "prudential considerations."[1]

The circumstances which induced the colonists of Massachusetts to manufacture their own coin, are briefly these:

King Charles I had shown plainly by his conduct that he regarded the colonists as exiles. His "Orders in Council" were overbearing and ruinous; and in time of danger and necessity he had afforded no assistance. As a consequence, on the division of sentiments between the king and the Parliament, the sentiments of the Pilgrims and Puritans were decidedly with the Reformers. Indeed in the contest between the King and the Reformers, the Pilgrims sent over "useful men"[2] to aid the reformation.

Charles was beheaded and Cromwell was soon

[1] Hutchinson, i, 164.

[2] John Leverett, afterwards Governor of Massachusetts, was one of these, and was appointed a Captain in Rainsborrow's regiment.

after made Lord Protector; and although the legislation of the Commonwealth threatened to be slightly unfavorable to the people of Massachusetts, in requiring a return of their charter for alterations which they feared would hazard their liberties, they were successful in their efforts to retain it unaltered.

The colonists, of course, sympathized heartily with the new Commonwealth, and in return, they were humored by the protection and favor of Cromwell. They felt that they were under little or no restraint from the home government, and they felt too that royalty was prostrate; hence legislation was carried on with a view to strengthen and build up their own Commonwealth.

The currency consisted heretofore, principally of the coins of England, Spain and Portugal. But the commerce which at first extended only to trade with the Indians, and to traffic among the other colonies, began to expand, and gradually considerable intercourse grew up with the West Indies. Through this channel, it is probable that much bullion was brought into the country. There was such a scarcity of genuine coin, however, that it was common to carry on trade by the transfer of skins, cattle, &c.[1]

The difficulties experienced in carrying on trade without a sufficient currency, were quite general with

[1] Musket balls, full bore, were a legal tender in Massachusetts in 1656, and were current for a farthing a piece, provided that no man be compelled to take above twelve at a time.—*Ackerman.*

the colonies in America, and the authorities of
Massachusetts made the first effectual movement to
obviate the inconvenience occasioned thereby, by an
act or order passed on the 27th day of May 1652,
which order provided for the establishment of a
mint and the coinage of shillings, sixpences
and threepences. The order prescribed[1] that NE
should be stamped on the side, and XII on the reverse of shillings, VI on sixpences, and III on three-
penny pieces. They were rudely shaped, (Pl. 1,
fig. 1, 2,) and in addition to the stamp above described, they had a private mint mark which was
designated every three months by the Governor and
the mint officers, and was known only to them.

The act directed also, that the aforesaid and no
other coins, except the English, should be acknowledged to be the current money of the Commonwealth.

In consideration of the importance of the project
to the community, and fearing lest it should not be
expeditiously carried out, the General Court appointed Richard Bellingham, William Hibbens, John Leverett and Thomas Clarke a committee to select a
situation for a mint-house, and to administer to the
master an oath, which was, that all money coined by
him should "be of the just alloy of the English
cojne; that every Shilling should be of due weight,
namely, Three-penny Troj weight, and all other
pieces proportionably, so neere as they could." The

1 See Appendix.

subordinate officers were to be appointed by this committee, who were likewise directed to determine what else should appear to them necessary, in order to carry out the order of the Court.

John Hull[1] of Boston was chosen the director of the mint, and he was to have about one shilling out of every twenty to pay him for his trouble.[2] He associated with him Robert Sanderson, as will appear by the following extract from the manuscript diary of said John Hull. It begins:

"1652. Also upon the occasion of much counterfeit coin brought into the country and much loss accruing in that respect, (and that did occasion a stoppage of trade,) the General Court ordered a mint to be set, and to coyne, bringing to the sterling standard for fineness and for weighte. They made choyse of me for that employment, and I chose my friend

[1] John Hull was a skillful silversmith and probably came to this country with his uncle or grandfather. It is not certain that his father ever came over. His grandfather, Robert Hull, was a blacksmith of Boston in 1637. John probably learned his trade before his emigration.—*Drake's Hist. Boston.*

[2] The mint master probably made handsome profits out of his business. The Court at one time attempted to release him from his contract by offering a large sum of money. When his daughter married Samuel Sewall, the founder of Newbury, Mass., he gave as her dowry the bride's weight in silver. It is said that when the wedding ceremony was ended, a large pair of scales was brought out and suspended. In one disk the blushing bride was placed, and pine tree shillings were poured into the other until there was an equipoise. The fortunate man married about one hundred and fifty thousand dollars.

Robert Sanderson to be my partner, to which the Court consented."[1]

The mint-house was ordered to be made of wood, to be sixteen feet square, and ten feet high, and to be erected upon the land of John Hull,[2] and in case of his removal, the said land was to be possessed by the Commonwealth, on the valuation of two commissioners to be chosen by the Commonwealth and Mr. Hull. The implements and tools necessary for carrying on the manufacture of coins having been procured, operations were commenced. All persons having bullion, plate or Spanish coin were allowed to bring it to the mint, and to be present while the same was being melted, refined and alloyed, and upon taking a receipt for the same from the mint master, they received the like weight in current money.

The irregular shape of the coins issued, and the fact that so small a part of the surface was impressed with the stamp, afforded excellent opportunities for

[1] John Mansfield of Charlestown petitioned the General Court in 1654 that he might help "to quine and melt and fine Siluer with Mr. Hull and Goodman Saunders in the country howse," and said "for I serued 11 years and ½ prentiz to the same arts, and am a free man of London, and am also sworne to be trew to the country, as I hope I shall."—*Felt.*

[2] His land is not described in the *Book of Possessions.* He died intestate, and after his death (which took place Sept. 29, 1683, he being 50 years of age) his estate was distributed between Judith, his widow, and his daughter Hannah, wife of Samuel Sewall. At the death of the widow, it was to be equally divided amongst the three children of Hannah Sewall.—*Drake's Boston.*

frauds, such as filing and clipping.[1] The authorities therefore, seasonably directed that the device
should be altered[2] to that of a double ring on
either side, with Massachusetts for an inscription,
and a tree in the centre. Ten years later[3] a two-
penny piece was ordered to be struck, corresponding
to the above description. (Pl. 1, fig. 3, 4, 5, 6.)

It is not absolutely certain that the pine was the
tree intended to have been represented on these
coins. While the mint was in operation the die must
have been frequently altered, the figure of the tree,
as appears by specimens now extant, having been
considerably varied. Many of these more closely
resemble the species of pine than any other tree
Mr. Felt[4] represents, that at all events, the pine
was a favorite symbol with the authorities of the
colony. It was appointed on the state flag April
11, 1776,[5] and it continued to the adoption of the
thirteen stripes, but what idea was connected with
the symbol, we can only conjecture. It is said that

[1] In Great Britain this practice was so extensive that the new
coinage which Charles II ordered on his restoration, before three
years were ended, so much diminished in value that 572 bags of
100 lbs. each, which should have weighed 221,419 oz. 16 pwts. 8
grs., yielded only 113,771 oz. 5 pwts.—*Fleetwood.*

[2, 3] See Appendix.

[4] Acct. of Mass. currency.

[5] By a proclamation of Governor Shirley of March 14, 1775, it
was ordered that one of the devices for stamped paper as a revenue
towards the support of our Government, should be a pine tree.

the ancient Britons used a coin with a pine tree on it, while they paid taxes to the Romans, which Camden supposes to have been money paid for assessment on wood land. The pine as used by our forefathers was more probably a sign of permanency[1] than of tributary subjection.[2]

The success of the minting operations, to the proprietors, did not escape notice. The General Court after having allowed them the free use of the mint-house for about eight years, appointed a committee to confer with Messrs. Hull & Sanderson as to the propriety of making an annual "meete honorarium" to the country, and in case of their refusal, to inform them that an agreement would be made with other parties to carry on the mint. The Mint masters not liking the alternative of this proposition, offered ten pounds as a bonus to the Commonwealth, but refused to make any agreement which should bind them to pay an annual rent. After advising with the Court, the committee accepted the ten pounds and the matter rested until the year 1667, when a committee was again appointed for a similar object and with like instructions.

[1] In a conference with Eastern Indians at Boston, January 12, 1714, "General Nicholson shewed them a New England Shilling with a pine tree thereon; saying, they and the English should be like that tree, but one root, though several branches; the pine tree is always green, an emblem of truth, and if the root be cut the branches dye."—*Felt*.

[2] Ibid.

After consultation with the proprietors, it was agreed, that in consideration of the expense which the government had from time to time incurred in constructing and repairing the mint buildings, the mint masters would pay into the general treasury, for the succeeding seven years, ten pounds annually, and within six months from the date of the agreement, forty pounds in addition.

But the difficulties experienced in trade on account of a want of money, had not altogether been overcome by the issues from the mint. Much of this coin found its way out of the country. To prevent loss in this respect it was enacted, that no coin of the colony, excepting twenty shillings to pay individual expenses, should be exported, under penalty of forfeiture of the whole estate of the transgressor. It was further enacted in 1672 that Spanish money should be current in the colony, but that all such money should be stamped at the mint with the letters N E and the exact weight of each piece.[1] The Court afterwards raised the value of these coins. Pieces-of-eight, as they were called, were rated at 6s. 8d. instead of 6s., if they weighed an ounce of silver, and the smaller pieces in proportion.

The time for which Messrs. Hull & Sanderson had been authorized to conduct the mint having expired, the General Court in 1675,[2] empowered the go-

[1] See Appendix.

[2] See Appendix.

2

vernor and resident magistrates of Boston to contract with such parties as they should deem proper,
to perform the coining for the colony. This committee was instructed to make such arrangements
as would be profitable and "encouraging to all persons that have bullion to bring in the colony to the
mint."

The committee renewed the contract with the
former mint masters to continue to coin for seven
years. The compensation was to remain the same,
viz : fifteen pence for every twenty shillings coined,
but the latter agreed to pay an annual rent of twenty
pounds into the treasury of the colony.

This new contract was made in the face of the fact
that the minting operations, far from having received
the royal approbation, had rather been criticised and
objected to. As attention from this quarter was now
being drawn to the subject, the colonists endeavored
variously to persuade the king of the innocence of
the proceeding, and of its value as well to himself
as to their commerce. They offered to waive any
preference they might have for the character or
description of the impress on the coins, and directed
their London agents to request his majesty to "order
such an impress as shall be to him most acceptable."

Both in 1685 and 1686 reports on the institution
were made by the officers of the London mint and
by the Lord High Treasurer of England, respectively.
The former complained of the lightness of the coins,

and the latter urged reasons why the establishment should be abolished.

The Massachusetts mint existed about thirty-four years,[1] the first date, 1652,[2] having been retained on the shilling, sixpenny and threepenny pieces, and 1662 on the two pence.[3] Although the establishment was not abandoned until about 1688, money was probably not coined there after the year 1686.[4]

After William and Mary came to the throne, the colonists again applied for the privilege of sustaining the Boston mint. Their petition does not appear to have been favorably received. But in this reign a copper coin was struck for New England, of the

[1] Oldmixon (British Empire in America, vol. I., p. 98) writes as though the Boston mint existed about the year 1706. This is an error.

[2] A collection in Salem, Mass., is said to contain a shilling with the date 1650. Coins of questionable dates may have been struck as patterns.

[3] In Earl Pembroke's celebrated collection was a coin having on the obverse, MASSACHVSETS IN., group of the Good Samaritan; above, FAC SIMILE; reverse, the same as on the shilling. It was ascertained after the death of the earl that the coin was spurious, having been altered from a pine tree shilling, by smoothing one side and stamping thereon the group above described.

[4] It is said that Charles II, during a conversation with Sir Thomas Temple (a) on the state of affairs in Massachusetts, expressed himself quite dissatisfied with the colonists on account of their infringement of his prerogative in coining money, and threatened their punishment. Upon Sir Thomas taking from his pocket a shilling

(a) Sir Thomas Temple resided several years in New England during the interregnum. After the restoration he returned to England.

following description: obverse, an ELEPHANT facing
the left; reverse, GOD PRESERVE NEW ENGLAND, 1694,
in five lines across the field.[1]   (Pl. 1, fig. 7.)

Large amounts of the Massachusetts money were
sent to England, in order to pay debts, and the difficulties occasioned by the scarcity of coin continually
increased rather than diminished. Indeed the matter
of currency appears to have been one of constant attention and experiment. The issuing of paper money
was also resorted to; in 1701 some individuals stamped
pieces of brass and tin, attempting to pass them at
a penny each, but they were soon obliged by the
authorities to withdraw them.[2]   In the same year
a committee of the General Court reported in
favor of issuing copper pence, but the Council did
not concur.[3]   Still intent on supplying to some
extent the public demand, the Court contracted in
1703 for the importation of £5000 worth of copper
pence. There appears however, to have been no considerable increase of the metalic currency of the colony of Massachusetts until the year 1749, when a large

stamped with the figure of the pine tree, the king asked what tree
it was? Sir Thomas told him that of course it was the Royal Oak
which had preserved his majesty's life; the king laughing called
them honest dogs, and permitted Sir Thomas to proceed with his
representation.—*Memoirs of Hollis.*

[1] In the description of the Beaufroy collection of coins, Mr. Burnt
notices these as belonging to the Anglo-American coins, and con-
cludes that the die was executed privately by the Roettiers, and not
engraved in the Tower mint.

[2] Felt.   [3] Ibid.

amount of coin was sent over from England on account of expenses incurred by the colonies in the expedition against Cape Breton. The Lords of the Treasury in their report on the subject, state the proportion of Massachusetts at £261,700. It was brought over under the care of Mr. William Bollan, the agent of the province, and consisted of 653,000 oz. of silver and 10 tons of copper, probably a larger amount of coin than had ever been in Massachusetts at one time. Such a remittance and others subsequent, gave this province the name of the "hard money colony."[1]

MARYLAND.

The colonists of Maryland from their earliest settlement suffered severely from the want of a proper circulating medium. Besides cattle and corn, powder and shot were common articles of currency, until Lord Baltimore after repeated solicitations undertook to provide a supply of coinage.[2] He had dies prepared in London, and sent over to his

[1] Felt.

[2] I have not been able to discover any grant to this nobleman of the privilege to coin money in express terms, but presume that he exercised it by virtue of general words in the charter which granted the Province of Maryland to him, and to his heirs, on the 20th of June, 1632. By that instrument he was to enjoy it with *omnia jura regalia* in as full and ample a manner as they had been heretofore enjoyed by the Bishop of Durham. Now as these prelates did for-

brother Philip Calvert and to the governor and council, specimens of the coins which he proposed to put in circulation.[1] The communications of his lordship which accompanied the specimens were read in council on the 3d of March, 1659-60, as will appear from the following extracts from the Council Records.[2]

"At a Council held at Bushwood, Mr. Slyes howse, in St. Mary's County, on Saturday the 3d of March 1659–60:

"Present—The Gov. Josias Fendall, Esq.; Philip Calvert, Esq., Secretary; Thomas Gerrard, Esquire, Coll. John Price, Robert Clarke, Esq., Col. Nathaniell Utye, Baker Brooke, Esq., Doctor Luke Barber.

"Then was read his L'd'ps Letter directed to his Lieutenant and Councell, dated 12th of October, and directed to the Secretary, touching the Mint, as followeth, viz :

"After my hearty commendations, &c. Having with great paines and charge, procured Necessaries for a particular coyne to be currant in Maryland, a sample whereof, in a peece of a shilling, a sixpence, and a groate, I herewith send you, I recommend it to you to promote all you can, the dispersing it, and by

merly possess the privilege of a mint, it whould seem that his Lordship availed himself of the general grant of legal rights, and as the power of coinage was not particularly excepted, exercised that together with the rest.—*Ruding.*

[1] S. F. Streeter, in Hist. Mag. Feb. 1858.

[2] Ibid.

Proclamation to make currant within Maryland, for all payments upon contracts or causes happening or arising after a day to be by you limited in the said Proclamation. And to procure an act of Assembly for the punishing of such as shall counterfeit the said Coyne, or otherwise offend in that behalfe, according to the form of an act recommended by me last year, to my Govenor and Secretary, or as neere it as you can procure from the Assembly and to give me your advice next year, touching what you think best to be further done in that matter touching coyne; for, if encouradgement be given by the good success of it this yeare there wil be abundance of adventurers in it the next yeare."

Only a few days after the receipt of this letter Gov. Fendall attempted to revolutionize the colony. The confusion occasioned thereby interrupted for a while the carrying out of the money scheme; but on Philip Calvert being appointed governor, he set about at once to procure the passage of an act for "the setting up of a mint within the Province of Maryland." Such an act was passed on the 1st of May, 1661. Adopting the recommendations of the Proprietor, the General Assembly enacted, that the money that should be coined for the province should be of as good silver as English sterling money, every shilling to weigh above nine pence, and other pieces in proportion. For counterfeiting, clipping or in any way diminishing the coin, the offender should suffer death and the forfeiture of lands, goods, &c., to the Ld Proprietor. His Lordship agreed to accept the said coin in payment of rents and all other engagements due him. The act doubtless contemplated the establishment of a mint in the province, as its title implies. Indeed his Lordship is requested to take order for the *setting up of a mint within the province of Maryland,*[1] and the act prescribes the weight and value of the money to be coined *therein.*

Ruding[2] also, states that the money was coined in Maryland, but he is incorrect in supposing it to to have been struck at an earlier date. But, from the statements in the letter above quoted, and in the absence of evidence to the contrary, it must be concluded that the mint for *coining* money was not established in Maryland.

Lord Baltimore proceeded directly to send an amount of coin sufficient to supply the immediate wants of the colonists. These coins had on the obverse, a profile bust of Lord Baltimore, legend, CÆCILIVS, DNS : TERRÆ : MARIÆ : & CT. Reverse, an escutcheon, with family arms, on either side the value of the coin[3] in numerals, legend, CRESCITE : ET : MVLTI-

[1] Appendix.

[2] Annals of Coinage, vol. I, p. 417.

[3] One variety of the shilling has the arms of his wife, a *cross bottannée* quartered, on the reverse. This coin which is supposed to be unique, was in the possession of the late Sir Frederick Morton Eden.—*Ruding.*

PLICAMINI. (Pl. 2, figs. 1, 2, 3). Immediately on the receipt of this currency the legislature passed an act to provide for its circulation. Every householder and freeman within the province was required " to take up ten shillings per poll of the said money for every taxable under their charge and custody, and pay for the same in good casked Tobacco, at 2d. per pound, to be paid upon tender of the said sums of money, proportionably for every such respective family."[1] Copper half-pennies with the same obverse as the pieces above described; reverse, DENARIVM: TERRÆ-MARIÆ: two flags on a ducal coronet, the Baltimore crest (Pl. 2, fig. 4), are occasionally found. They are exceedingly scarce, and were probably struck only as patterns.[2]

As in Massachusetts, an adequate supply of money was not speedily obtained. The currency continued in a state of great disorder, which was a matter of much complaint, and the trade of the province was greatly impeded thereby. Various suggestions, experiments and orders were made, and the Assembly in 1686 enacted, that New England shillings and sixpences should pass as sterling (at an advance of 3d. in each shilling). French crowns, pieces-of-eight and rix dollars to pass at 6s., ducatoons at 7s. 6d.,

[1] Bacon's Laws, 1662, April 12.

[2] Mr. Thorsby mentions a groat of the same mint, and a copper coin of the same place, like the shilling with VI, which no doubt was the stamp of the sixpence, for I have seen that of the shilling likewise in copper.—*Leake's Coins.*

3

and all coins of silver or gold to be taken with the
advance of 3d. sterling, in the value of 12d. sterling.
Later than this, tobacco was made a legal tender, at
one penny per pound, and Indian corn at twenty
cents per bushel, and last of all, notwithstanding its
experienced insufficiency in other parts, paper money
was resorted to.

CAROLINA.

In Carolina, as a British province, it is probable that a very small amount, if any special coinage
was ever in circulation. A coin was issued in the
reign of William and Mary, probably simultaneously
with one struck for New England, and which it will
be observed it very closely resembles. It is described as follows: obverse, an Elephant; reverse, GOD
PRESERVE CAROLINA, AND THE LORDS PROPRIETORS,
1694, in six lines across the field.[1] (Pl. 1, fig. 8).
Sterling money was the legal money of the country,
but unfortunately there was quite as little of it here
as in any of the other colonies.

Arthur Dobbs, governor of North Carolina in 1753,
sent over to the treasury department a proposal to
coin copper money for that colony, to consist of
pieces of the value of two-pence, one penny and a
half-penny of their currency, which was in proportion to that of England as four to three. He proposed that the quantity to be coined, should be de-

[1] See note, page 12.

termined by the Governor and Council, but not to exceed fifty tons: that they should deliver the copper into the mint, pay all expenses and fees attending the coinage, and to have such a device upon the coins as should be thought proper. This proposal was sent down from the treasury to the officers of the mint for their consideration, who suggested that one half of what should be coined should be in half-pence, of such a size as that sixty-one pieces should make a pound avoirdupois; that one-fourth should consist of two-penny pieces, and the other fourth, of penny pieces, of a proportioned weight to the half-pence: that the coinage should be performed at the same price as that for Ireland, viz: five pence per pound for the master, and twenty shillings per hundred for the comptroller. One side of the coin to have the king's effigy with GEORGIUS II REX; on the reverse, the arms of North Carolina, inscribed, SEPT. CAROLINA, and under it the date of the year. It is believed that this proposal was never carried into execution.[1]

NEW HAMPSHIRE.

The province of New Hampshire continued down to the period of the Revolution to be governed by a commission, but enacted her own laws through a general assembly. In providing for the credit of the Province, she pursued the same course as that adopted by the other colonies, and with no better

[1] Ruding.

success. Her paper currency became worthless, but
she furnishes us the only record of an attempt to
exchange a paper for a copper currency. The house
of representatives on the 28th of June, 1776, voted,
that the treasurer of the colony should receive into
the treasury in exchange for the paper bills of the
colony any quantity of copper coin made in the
colony, of the weight of five pennyweight and ten
grains each, to the amount of any sum not exceeding
£1,000 lawful money, three of which coppers should
be received and paid for two-pence, in all payments.
These coins were to have the following device, &c.,
viz: A pine tree, with the words AMERICAN LIBERTY
on one side, and a harp and the date 1776, on the
other.[1] The resolution was never carried into effect.

VIRGINIA.

The same charter which granted the territories
commonly called Virginia, covered also what became
subsequently known as the territories of the Plymouth Company. The associates of Sir Thomas
Gates, the original grantee, were divided into two
companies. The name of Virginia became gradually applied to those who formed the South Colony,
while the north settlement assumed the name of the
Plymouth Company.

It was in the South Colony, or Virginia, that the
earliest movement was made in America, to establish

[1] American Archives, 5th Series, v. 1.

a colonial mint. In 1645, seven years earlier than the Massachusetts authorities had made provision for a metallic currency of their own, the grand assembly of Virginia having "maturely[1] weighed and considered how advantageous a quoine current would be to this collony, and the great wants and miseries which do daily happen unto it by the sole dependency upon tob'o, Resolved, that a quoine of copper would be most beneficial to, and with most ease procured by the collony," and enacted a law establishing a mint and coinage, accordingly. All persons were thereby directed "to leave off trading for tob'o," under penalty of forfeiture of the article so bought or sold.

The law contemplated the purchase, at the public expense, of ten thousand pounds of copper as a stock, which was to be divided among those who should be constituted a company to coin the same. For the mintage, 12d. per pound was allowed. The copper coinage thus provided for, was to consist of two, three, six and nine-penny pieces. The only device prescribed, was that "upon every piece of coyne there be two rings, the one for the motto, the other to receive a new impression, which shall be stampted yearly, with some new figure, by one appointed for that purpose in each county." Capt. John Upton was confirmed as mint master, but the appointment of other officers, as well as the regulation of the affairs of the mint, was entrusted to Gov. Sir Wm. Berkeley. It is evident that this enactment was never carried into effect.

[1] See Appendix.

It is not absolutely certain that the colony of Virginia had at any time a currency of its own.[1] In the time of George III, a copper coin of the following description was struck, obverse, the head of George III, legend, GEORGUIS III REX; reverse, a shield in quarters, containing respectively, the arms of England, Scotland, Ireland and the Electoral Dominions. It is about the size of an English half-penny, and a well executed piece (Plate 2, No. 7). It probably had no very considerable circulation.

COINAGE OF THE COLONIES AT LARGE.

In the frequent representations of the trade of the plantations, the attention of the home governments was repeatedly directed to the inconveniences occasioned as well by the different valuations attached to the same coins in different localities as by the baseness of the money itself. The Spanish, British and Dutch coins were those principally in circulation in America. The vast importance of the British settlements in America became well understood, and the frequent appeals made by the colonists for relief in the matter of currency were not unheeded, although it was at no very early date that the assistance of the proper authorities was granted.

On the 5th of July, 1700, the board of trade took into consideration the state of coin in the plantations.

[1] " In Virginia, copper coins have never been in use."—*Jefferson's Writings,* v. 2, I. 136.

A memorial by Mr. John Fysack was then read, proposing the erection of a mint in some of the plantations on the continent of America, as a means of remedying many inconveniences in the trade of those parts Their lordships did not think fit that any mint should be erected there, but they resolved at some convenient opportunity to consider the difficulties arising therein. It is not probable, however, that they proceeded further, for in 1707, the practice of different valuations still continued, notwithstanding a proclamation against it, which had been issued in 1704.[1]

In the reign of George I a new species of coins was struck. It is believed to be the only issue for general circulation ever authorized by the British government, for the use of the British American colonies. They were made of a mixed metal resembling brass, and were of three sizes, one nearly as broad as a half-crown, another about the size of an English half-penny, and a third about the size of a farthing, all bearing the same stamp, viz : obverse his majesty's head. The larger pieces had this legend, GEORGIUS D. G. MAG. BRI. FRA. ET HIB. REX. On the smaller pieces this inscription was abridged to GEORGIUS DEI GRATIA REX; reverse a large double rose ; legend, ROSA AMERICANA, UTILI DULCI, 1722 or 1723. (Pl. 5.)

The inscription on the smallest piece, is merely GEORGIUS D. G. REX, reverse, ROSA AMERI : UTILE DULCI, 1722.

[1] Ruding's Annals.

Those with the date of 1723 have the rose crowned. (Pl. 5.)

These coins were manufactured by William Wood, who, according to the author of "a Defence of the conduct of the people of Ireland in their unanimous refusal of Mr. Wood's copper money," obtained a patent for coining small money for the English plantations, in pursuance of which he had the conscience to make thirteen shillings out of a pound of brass. According to Snelling,[1] others were concerned in the scheme. Kingsmill Eyres, Mr. Marsland, a hard-ware man in Cornhill, and several more. The dies were engraved by Mr. Lammas, Mr. Standbroke, and Mr. Harold, some of which were in the possession of Mr. Winthorpe, who went to New York. They were made of Bath metal,[2] and struck at the French change, in Hog lane, Seven Dials, by an engine that raised and let fall a heavy weight upon them when made hot.

The speculation and its fate are thus alluded to in the 3d of the *Drapier's* letters, written by Swift in 1724: "He (Wood) has already tried his faculty in New England, and I hope he will meet, at least, with an equal reception here. What that was I leave to public intelligence."

The influence[3] of government was brought to bear on New England, in the hope that it would receive the coin, and the Duke of Newcastle, then at the head

1 View of the coins struck for the West India Colonies, 39.

2 Snelling.

3 Doc. Hist. N. Y., v. 3.

of the Board of Trade, wrote to Lt. Gov. Dummer in October 1725, informing him of the authenticity of Wood's patent for coining half-pence, pence and two-pence, "for the use of his majesty's dominions in America," and recommending the patentee to the favor of the Massachusetts colony. But we presume that the scheme was a failure, as well in New England, as in Ireland, for the author of the Defence already quoted, says "the money was rejected in a manner not so decent as that of Ireland,"[1] whilst Marsland, the Cornhill hard-ware man, had such

[1] As the fate of Wood's coinage in Ireland has been alluded to, it will not be out of place here, to give a short account of it. The privilege was granted in 1722, and was to continue 14 years, and the quantity to be coined was limited to 360 tons. By artful misrepresentations the measure became extremely unpopular in Ireland. It was charged that notorious frauds and deceits had been committed by the patentee. Dean Swift attacked it from the pulpit and the press. In his *Works* he is represented as having said that he never preached but twice in his life, and then they were not sermons but pamphlets. Being asked on what subject? he replied, they were against Wood's half-pence. Only one of the sermons is extant, and of that, Ruding says, "it is compounded of mistatement, exageration and falsehood." Such was the influence, however, of his harangues and of his *Drapier's Letters** that addresses from the authorities of Ireland, from the lowest to the highest, were presented against the money, and the grand jury of Dublin, presented as enemies to the government, all such persons as had attempted or *should endeavor* to impose Wood's half-pence upon them. Notwithstanding an investigation by the lords of the privy council, which resulted in exonerating Wood, the outcry against him continued, and he was obliged at last to resign his patent.†

* A reward of £300 was offered by the Government for the discovery of the author of Drapier's 4th letter.

† Ruding.

4

quantities of it in his cellar, that he was ruined by it. He died house-keeper of Gresham College.[1] It is probable, however, that though discarded in New England, it circulated in some of the other colonies, as some specimens have been found as far south as Virginia, and even as Charleston, S. C.[2]

Another coin of the same description as the last was struck in the time of George II, 1733. It is rarely met with, and was probably a pattern.

Sir Alex. Cumming in 1748, presented a memorial to parliament, in which he proposed, that in order to preserve the dependence of the British plantations in America, on Great Britain, the current specie of Great Britain should be made the current, lawful money of the said plantations, and that £200,000 sterling be coined in the Tower, for that purpose, which sum was to be made the foundation of a provincial bank for the British plantations in America, in order to abolish the paper currency of New England and Carolina. The proposition was not adopted.[3]

[1] Snelling's view.
[2] Mass. Hist. Soc., VII, 283.
[3] Ruding.

CHAPTER II.

COINS OF THE PERIOD OF THE CONFEDERATION.

From the period which closed with the last chapter, to that which opens with the present, covering the years of the great struggle for Independence, the annals of American coinage are confined to a few private and unauthorized issues.

During the time of the Confederation, from 1778 to 1787, the right of coining money was entrusted to the individual states as well as to the general government. The privilege was exercised to a considerable extent, generally in the manufacture of copper cents and half cents. Grants for this purpose were made by Vermont in June 1785, by Connecticut in October 1785, by New Jersey in June 1786, by Massachusetts in October 1786. The first coinage by order of the Congress of the Confederation was issued in the latter part of the year 1787.

VERMONT.

The legislature of Vermont, at the June session, 1785, granted to Reuben Harmon, jr.,[1] of Rupert,

---

[1] Reuben Harmon, jr. came, according to the relation of Mr. Julian Harmon, his son, from Suffield, Conn., according to another authority he came from Sandisfield, Mass. He accompanied his father,

the exclusive right to coin copper money within that state, for two years after the first day of July following.   Mr. Harmon had already procured a quantity of copper suitable for coinage, and had perhaps intended to manufacture coppers without proper authority, but he found no difficulty in procuring the approval of his project by the general assembly, and a committee was appointed to cooperate with him in the details of the undertaking. He was required to give bonds to the amount of £5000 for the faithful performance of his contract, and no coin manufactured by him was to weigh less than one-third of an ounce, Troy weight.

After much expense incurred in buildings, Harmon succeeded in getting his works in operation.   The mint-house was located near the north-east corner of the town of Rupert, a little east of the main road leading from Dorset to Pawlet, on a small stream of water, called Mill brook, which empties into Pawlet river. It was a small building about sixteen by eighteen feet, made of rough materials, simply clapboarded, unplained and unpainted.   At the east end was the furnace for melting the copper, and machinery for rolling

and settled in the northeast part of Rupert, somewhere about the year 1768.   He was a merchant, and a man of some note and influence, having held the office of member of the general assembly, and of justice of the peace from 1780 to about 1790, besides several minor offices.   In the year 1800 he left Rupert, for that part of the state of Ohio called the Salt Spring Track, in Wethersfield township, Trumbull county, Ohio, where he was engaged in the manufacture of salt up to the time of his death, which event took place Oct. 29, 1806, when he was 56 years of age.

the bars, in the middle of the room that for cutting,
and at the west end was the machinery for stamping.
This was done by means of an iron screw; attached
to heavy timbers above, and moved by hand with the
aid of ropes. Sixty coppers per minute could be
stamped, although thirty per minute was the usual
number. The building was still standing in 1855,
but its location, &c. was entirely changed, it having
long since been removed to the edge of the adjoining town of Pawlet, where it is used as a corn
house.

The coins issued from this mint were of the following description: obverse, a sun rising from behind the
hills, and a plough in the foreground, legend, VER-
MONTENSIUM RES PUBLICA, 1786, reverse, a radiated
eye, surrounded by thirteen stars, legend, QUARTA
DECIMA STELLA. (Pl. 2, fig. 9).

In October 1786 Mr. Harmon, on the ground that
in the short time granted him, he would be unable
to indemnify himself in the expense he had incurred
in the beginning of his enterprise, applied for an
extension of his privilege for eight years from July
1787.

The assembly, willing to encourage an undertaking
that promised considerable public utility, under certain regulations and restrictions granted such an
extension, requiring the same amount of bonds as
under the previous contract. The coppers which he
coined were to weigh not less than four pennyweights
and fifteen grains each, and were to bear the following device: on one side, a head, with the motto

AUCTORITATE VERMONTENSIUM, abridged, and on the reverse a woman, with the letters INDE. ET LIB. for independence and liberty. (Pl. 3, fig. 2.) A few half cents were issued under this authority.

On the 7th of June, 1787, Harmon's firm, which consisted of himself and William Coley of Bennington county, Vt., Elias Jackson, of Litchfield, Conn., and Daniel Voorhis, goldsmith of New York, formed a partnership with another company, consisting of Thomas Machin,[1] Samuel Atlee, James F. Atlee, David Brooks, James Grier and James Giles, all of New York city, for the said term of eight years, for the coinage of coppers. By the first of July the New York firm were required by the terms of the copartnership "to complete at their own cost the works

[1] Capt. Machin was an officer of the American army. He was born on the 20th of March, 1744, near Wolverhampton, Staffordshire, England, and came to America in 1772, making his first residence at New York, but soon after removed to Boston, and was one of the Boston tea party of 1773. He acted as lieutenant, and was wounded at the battle of Bunker Hill. He received his first commission as second lieutenant in Col. Knox's regiment of artillery, Jan. 18, 1776. During the revolution he rendered important assistance in engineering. He superintended the construction and stretching of the great iron chain across the Hudson river, from Pollopel's island to the west bank. In 1779 he took the water level between Albany and Schenectady, with the view of supplying the former city with water, and submitted a plan for that object to the corporation. He married in Aug. 1782, a daughter of James Van Nostrand, of Huntington, L. I. He was commissioned captain by Gov. Clinton, to take rank as such from Aug. 21, 1780. In 1783 he settled at New Grange, Ulster county, N. Y., and afterwards removed to the town of Mohawk, and died at Charleston(a) April 3d, 1816.

(a) Charleston, Glen, and a part of Root, were formed from the town of Mohawk.

then erecting at the mills of the said Thomas Machin near the great pond, in the county of Ulster," while the other firm agreed in the same time to complete the works at Rupert, Bennington county, Vt. The ten partners divided the affairs of the company between them and agreed to meet on the first day of February, June and October of each year at Rhinebeck, N. Y., for the purpose of general business.[1]

It is supposed that William Coley, who had been a goldsmith in the city of New York, but who afterwards removed to Rupert, cut the dies and assisted in striking the coppers. He was at all events actively engaged in the operations. How long the Vermont money was coined, or the quantity that was manufactured is not known, but it is not improbable that other coppers were struck at the same mints.

For the privilege granted by the legislature to Mr. Harmon, he was required after three years of the eight had expired, to pay into the treasury of the state two and one-half per cent on the amount of the copper coin he should manufacture during the remainder of the term. The first three years he was allowed the use of the patent without any compensation to the state.

At the time the British in Canada were carrying on negociations with the leading men in Vermont, for the purpose of making Vermont a crown dependency, coppers were issued having on the obverse, 1, a bust of George III, legend, VERMON AUCTORI, reverse, the figure of Britannia; 2, obverse, a bust of George

[1] Simms's Hist. Schoharie county.

III., legend, GEORGIUVS III, VTS., reverse, a figure of Britannia, legend not intelligible. They were usually struck over British half-pennies.

CONNECTICUT.

Connecticut was the second state under the confederation that provided for a copper currency of her own. Vermont preceded her in legislation on this subject by only four months. At a session of the general assembly held in 1785, a memorial was presented by Samuel Bishop, Joseph Hopkins, James Hillhouse and John Goodrich for permission to establish a mint to coin money for the state of Connecticut. On the 20th of October permission was granted, and the memorialists were authorized to manufacture coppers to an amount not exceeding ten thousand pounds sterling.

The grantees on the 12th of the ensuing month formed a copartnership with Pierpont Edwards, Jonathan Ingersoll, Abel Buel[1] and Elias Shipman

---

[1] One of the most ingenious men of his time, a native of the town of Killingworth, Conn. His ingenuity was often turned to no good purpose. At an early age he was detected in altering a five shilling colony note to five pounds, for which offence he was imprisoned, cropped and branded. The tip of his ear only was cropped off; it was held on his tongue to keep warm until it was put on the ear again, where it grew on. Afterwards he constructed a lapidary machine, probably the first used in this country. Bernard Romans, who was constructing a map of North America, employed him to make a survey of the coast of Pensacola, and he assisted also in engraving the map. During the revolution he constructed a type foundry at New Haven, employing 15 or 20 boys in making types. Returning from a visit

under the name of the Company for Coining Coppers, holding equal shares, and under equal obligations to conform to the regulations of the act of incorporation.

The weight and description of the pieces were defined by statute. Six pennyweights was the required amount of copper in each, and the impression and inscription directed, were the following: obverse, a head, and for a circumscription the words AUCTORI CONNEC ; on the reverse, a female figure, the emblem of liberty, holding in her hand an olive branch; legend, INDE. ET LIB. 1785. (Pl. 3, fig. 3.)

For the term of five years, which was the time the grant was to continue, the proprietors of the mint were required to pay semi-annually into the state treasury one-twentieth part of all the coppers which should be manufactured.[1]

Roger Sherman, James Wadsworth, David Austin, Ebenezer Chittenden and Isaac Beers, were a board under the general assembly to inspect and approve the coppers before they were put in circulation. This board inspected, during the three years that the mint was in operation, twenty-eight thousand nine hundred and forty-four pounds weight of coined

to England, he erected one of the first cotton factories in New England. He died in the New Haven alms-house.

[1] A few years later, when a committee of the general assembly reported on the affairs of the company, it appeared that the state had received thirteen hundred and eighty-six pounds and one ounce of coined copper, equal at eighteen for one shilling, to £184 16s ¼d, and that there was a balance due the state of sixty-one pounds two ounces, equal to £8 3s.

copper, and the company subsequently testified that they had not put into circulation any coppers, except they had been inspected.

Ample protection was thrown around the parties interested in this enterprise, a law having been passed at the same session at which the mint was authorized, prohibiting any person to coin coppers without license. The company, with some prospect at all events of success, commenced operations.

In April 1786, James Jarvis became a partner, he having purchased the interest of Edwards and Shipman and a part of that of Mr. Ingersol. The company soon met with an obstacle in not being able to command a supply of stock, and for want of this insufficiency, they were obliged some time during the ensuing summer to suspend operations. On the 10th of September of the same year, under a bond to conform to the act of the legislature, they leased the mint to Mark Leavenworth for six weeks, or so many days in addition as the works should be useless by reason of the failure of any of the implements. These individuals carried on the manufacture for about eight weeks. They afterwards purchased shares of the company's stock, and on the 1st of November 1786 the several partners decided upon a new plan of operations, which was that they would conduct the mint separately, for certain periods of time to be agreed upon.

No new interest appears to have been admitted into the firm; changes were frequently made in the division of the shares until June 1787, when the company ceased to carry on the business. In the fall of 1788, Maj. Eli Leavenworth made at the mint blank coppers, which he procured to be stamped in New York with various impressions, some few of them with an impression similar to that on the coppers coined by the original company.

The general assembly at the January session, 1789, appointed James Wadsworth and Daniel Holbrook a committee "to inquire into the conduct of those persons who were by a resolve of the Assembly in October 1785, authorized to coin and manufacture copper." The committee organized and notified the parties to meet at Mr. John Smith's house in New Haven on the 7th of April, 1789. Samuel Bishop, James Hillhouse and Mark Leavenworth appeared and were examined. The result was a full exposition of the affairs of the company from its organization. No frauds or other serious matters were proved, except that a small balance of per centage on the coppers coined, was found to be due to the state.

The following were the owners and the amounts of their respective shares, at the time the company ceased coining coppers for Connecticut.

James Jarvis,............. $\frac{4}{8}$ & $\frac{1}{16}$ parts.

James Hillhouse, ... $\frac{1}{8}$ part.

Mark Leavenworth,............. $\frac{1}{8}$ part.

Abel Buel,.................... $\frac{1}{8}$ part.

John Goodrich,............... $\frac{1}{16}$ part.

It is altogether probable that other coppers were coined by individuals of this company, at this mint.

NEW JERSEY.

The manufacture of coppers in the state of New Jersey appears to have been founded upon the suggestions and operations of Walter Mould. Mr. Mould had been employed in Birmingham, Eng., in an establishment where coppers were manufactured; and as the currency of the country, and the scarcity of money were much talked about in New Jersey as elsewhere, he communicated to his friends his knowledge of the process of coining, and proposed to manufacture a certain amount of copper money, if the proper authority should be obtained.

At the suggestion of Silas Condict, he applied to the legislature for permission to coin money. He had brought with him to this country many of his tools and implements of trade, and he therefore represented, that in the construction of the necessary manufactory, but little time would be lost. The application of the petitioners, Walter Mould, Thomas Goodsby and Albion Cox, having been referred to a committee and considered, was favorably reported upon to the legislature, and on the 1st of June, 1786, an act was passed, authorizing the petitioners to coin coppers. This act authorized their manufacture to an amount equal in value to £10,000, fifteen coppers to the shilling; each coin to be of pure copper, and to weigh six pennyweights and six grains. The justices of the supreme court, or any of them, were to direct what inscription, &c., should be placed on the coin. Heavy bonds were required from the contractors, that within two years from the publication of the act, the said amount of £10,000 in coppers should be coined; that one-tenth of this amount so coined should be delivered quarterly to the state treasurer for the use of the state. The patent thus granted was an exclusive one. All other persons were prohibited from coining money in New Jersey without a grant from the legislature, under penalty of twelve pounds for each day's offence.

On the 22d of November of the same year, Thomas Goodsby and Albion Cox were authorized to coin two-thirds of the amount of the coinage above contemplated, and Walter Mould one-third. The object of this proceeding was to secure to the state the full benefit of the former act, which it was thought might be defeated by the parties being bound jointly to execute the contract. It is not improbable, however, that a want of agreement between the parties as first constituted, had somewhat to do with this new arrangement. At a subsequent session (June, 1787), an act was passed for the benefit of the contractors, by which a penalty was imposed upon any one who should offer to pass coppers other than those coined under the authority of the state of New Jersey, or which might be issued by the United States Congress.

From the dates on the pieces, it appears that coppers were coined during 1786, 1787 and 1788. There can be little doubt but that there were two establishments in use for the purpose. Mould's cop-

pers were manufactured in his own house at a place
known as Solitude, about two miles west of Mor-
ristown, on the turnpike leading to Sussex Court
House. Mr. Cox and one Gilbert Rindle, conducted
their coinage at Elizabeth, in a building occupied
by the widow of Col. Matthias Ogden, of the Re-
volutionary army, and adjoining the residence
of Col. Francis Barber. The business was carried
on in a room behind the kitchen. In the middle of
this room a pit was sunk, several feet deep, and in
the center of the pit the die was stationed, the top
of which was about level with the floor of the room.
A workman seated himself on the edge of the pit,
and, placing smooth coppers on the die, dropped
them when stamped into the pit. The impression
was made by a screw press which was worked by
two men, one at each end of a horizontal lever
which was attached to the screw at the center of its
length. The lever was nine or ten feet in length.

The coppers of the New Jersey mint are described
as follows: Obverse, a horse's head, beneath which a
plough, legend, Nova Cæsarea, 1786, &c. ; reverse,
a shield, legend, E. Pluribus Unum.

MASSACHUSETTS.

The establishment of the Massachusetts mint of
1786, was not considered at the time a matter of
any great importance. It appears to have excited

very little interest, and no public discussion.[1] Probably in no other state was there existing so great a commotion on account of the derangement of the finances, and the scarcity of reliable currency. The attention of the legislature of that session, was mainly taken up in attempting to quiet disorders growing out of these causes. The mint was established more because it would have the appearance at least, of attempting to alleviate the public inconveniences, than from any important service that it was expected would be rendered by it. This view of the case is strengthened by the fact, that provision was made for coining only a small amount of copper, although the act contemplated as well the coinage of silver and gold. It was expected too, that congress would soon take active proceedings in the matter of a national currency. It had already, in 1782, approved of the establishment of a mint, in 1785 had fixed the money unit, and in 1786 had regulated the alloy and value of coin. The delegates from that body therefore, having learned that the subject of coinage was under consideration in the legislature of Massachusetts, suggested, that as provision would soon be made for the issue of an adequate supply of uniform currency, and as public confidence would be greater in a national coinage than in that of the separate states, a new issue by Massachusetts uuder such circumstances, would scarcely

[1] Neither in the governor's speech at the opening of the session, nor in the address from the legislature to the people, made at the close of the session, is any mention made of the mint.

be productive of much good. An act was nevertheless passed on the day succeeding the passage of a
similar ordinance by congress. The proceedings
of congress were of course not known to the legislature of Massachusetts.

On the 8th of March, 1786, Seth Reed presented a
petition praying to be licensed to coin copper and
silver money.[1] The matter having been referred, in
order that inquiry might be made into the expedi-
ency of coining money, on the 11th of October, the
committee having the subject in charge, reported
"that it would be highly advantageous to the commonwealth to erect a mint at Boston for the coining
of gold, silver and copper." Two days after, a bill
was introduced for such an object.

At this date, Rufus King having arrived in Boston
from congress, was invited by the members of the
house of representatives to appear before them and
give information relative to the affairs of the United
States, affecting the interests of the commonwealth.
He complied on the 12th of October. Among other
things he stated, " that the alloy and value of coins
having been established by congress, a mint would
probably soon be erected, and a coin with an American impression relieve the citizens under their dis-
tresses arising from the want of money." Within
two days, however, we find that the bill already
introduced was passed to be engrossed by the house
of representatives, and on the 17th of October,
1786, it was enacted that a mint should be esta-

[1] Massachusetts Records.

blished within the Commonwealth of Massachusetts,
for the coinage of gold, silver and copper, and that
each piece should bear the same name as was established by the resolve of Congress. The only ab-
solute provision for coinage, however, was, that
seventy thousand dollars' worth of cents and half
cents should be struck in copper, with such devices
and inscriptions as the Governor and Council should
approve. To the same authority was intrusted the
carrying out of the details of this measure, to provide suitable apparatus for the purpose of coining,
the appointment of mint officers and workmen, the
examination and auditing of all accounts.

In the spring of the year 1787, Joshua Witheral
was empowered to have the necessary buildings and
machinery provided. The works were erected on
Boston Neck and at Dedham. A resolve allowing
£600 for expenses to be incurred under the act, had
been passed October 23, 1786.

During the next year the coins were issued. On
the obverse was the American Eagle, having a bundle of arrows in its right talon, and in its left an
olive branch, a shield on its breast, with the word
CENT; legend, MASSACHUSETTS, 1788;[1] reverse, an
Indian holding a bow and arrow; legend, COMMON-
WEALTH and a star.

Only a few thousand dollars' worth of money was
manufactured, a portion of which amount was made
into half cents of the same description. (Pl. 3, fig. 5, 6.)

[1] Copies of this cent with the date 1787 are occasionally found.

UNITED STATES—CONFEDERATION.

The subject of a national mint for the United States, was first introduced by Robert Morris, the patriot and financier of the Revolution. As head of the finance department, he was instructed by Congress to prepare a report on the foreign coins then in circulation in the United States.

On the 15th of January, 1782, he laid before Congress an exposition of the whole subject. Accompanying this report was a plan for an American coinage, which it is claimed, originated with Gouverneur Morris,[1] who was assistant or deputy superintendent of Finance.

The financier, after noticing the inconveniences and disadvantages occasioned by the different values attached to the pound, the shilling and the penny in the various states, and deprecating the fact, that so many different coins were in circulation, considered that it was by no means of such importance to establish the relative value of different coins, as to provide a standard of our own, by which they might be estimated; and hence he urged the necessity of adopting an American coinage. He noticed the systems of coinage in foreign countries, and the principles which should be established in regulating

[1] There was no relationship of family between Robert Morris and Gouverneur Morris, at least, none that could be traced by them. Robert Morris was born in England, and came to America when he was thirteen years old.—*Sparks' Life of Gouverneur Morris.*

our own. He[1] recommended that the *money unit*
should be very small, and that money should be increased in a decimal ratio, which would afford easy
calculation. He did not urge that the unit should
be exactly represented in a coin, but as its value
would be precisely known, a number of units might
be represented in the lowest copper coin, which
might contain eight units, the next five, and called
respectively an EIGHT and a FIVE. A quarter of a
grain of fine silver in coined money would equal the
money unit, and proceeding as he suggested, in a
decimal ratio, one hundred would be the lowest silver coin, and might be called a CENT. "It would
contain twenty-five grains of fine silver, to which
might be added two grains of copper, and the whole
would weigh one pennyweight and three grains.
Five of them would make a QUINT, or five hundred
units, weighing five pennyweights and fifteen grains;
and ten would make a MARK, or one thousand units,
weighing eleven pennyweights and six grains." He
proposed also that there should be a CROWN,[2] of gold,
and other coins which should contain a precise
number of the money unit.

A considerable amount of public copper was then

[1] According to Jefferson this report was written entirely by Gouverneur Morris. Indeed the manuscript estimates and plans still
exist in his hand writing.

[2] This name he suggested on account of the following idea of an
impression for a gold coin, viz: An Indian with his bow in his left
hand, and in his right hand thirteen arrows, his foot on a *crown*; and
for an inscription, MANUS INIMICA TYRANNIS.

lying unappropriated at Philadelphia, and Mr. Morris assured congress, that if the plan for coining money was approved, he would immediately establish a mint, as machinery for that purpose could be easily constructed, and persons found who could carry on the necessary operations.

The letter of the superintendent of finance was referred to a committee consisting of one delegate from each state, who subsequently reported; and congress on the 21st of February, 1782, approved of the establishment of a mint, and directed the superintendent to prepare and report a plan for the same. He did not, however, do so, but in April, 1783, he inclosed to the president of congress specimens of coinage " with a view that if that body should think proper to appoint a committee on the subject, he might confer with them and explain his ideas of the plan of establishing and conducting a mint," and suggested that such a plan when reported by a committee, would more probably meet the ideas of congress than any which he might prepare.

The subject remained in this state for another year, congress being much occupied in devising plans for the pay of the army, &c. Mr. Morris having in the mean time resigned, Thomas Jefferson, in behalf of a committee appointed in 1784 to consider the subject of an American coinage, went over the whole field anew, reviewing and partially adopting Mr. Morris's views. His idea of the money unit he did not adopt, believing that it could not be practically adopted, and even if it should be,

would be decidedly inconvenient, on account of the
number of figures required to express a small
amount.[1] The dollar he adopted as his money unit,
and applied to it Mr. Morris's plan of decimal nota-
tion. Congress having heard a report from the

[1] Mr. Morris in a letter to Dr. Ramsay, a member of the Board of
Treasury, subsequently modified his plan, adopting a larger unit.
His idea was to have a money of account, and a money of coinage.
"He assumed for his unit an amount equal to twelve shillings and
sixpence sterling, which he called a pound, making this divisible
by ten, and giving the names of pounds, shillings, pence and doits
to the several divisions, thus :

One pound equal to	1,000
One shilling " "	100
One penny " "	10
One doit " "	1

Now, the money of all the states, reduced to pence, may be expressed in this doit, without a remainder. For example, in the
New England currency, five doits make a penny ; hence, £10 : 9 : 5,
reduced to pence, are equal to 2,633, which, multiplied by 5, give
13,165 doits, or 13 pounds and 165 doits of the new reckoning ; or
13 pounds, 1 shilling, 6 pence, 5 doits. By an easy process the
same result will follow with all the old currencies of the states ; that
is, any sum in pence may be reduced to doits without a fractional
remainder, which is rarely the case with the cents now in use. The
above unit is therefore taken, on account of its being susceptible of
this division.

It will be seen that, by omitting the names of shillings and pence,
the mode of reckoning will be by dollars and doits, precisely like
the present mode of dollars and cents, except that the place of doits
takes three figures instead of two. By rejecting the last figure,
as we now do the mills in common calculations, the reckoning
would then stand in dollars and pence, and be exactly the same
as the present mode.

The table of coins proposed in connection with this system of
reckoning was as follows :

committee to whom Mr. Jefferson's paper had been referred, in 1785 adopted this plan, and in 1786 decided upon the following names and characters of the coins : An EAGLE, to contain $246\frac{268}{1000}$ grains of fine gold, equal to ten dollars ; a HALF EAGLE, to contain $123\frac{134}{1000}$ grains of fine gold, equal to five dollars—these two coins to be stamped with the impression of the American Eagle ; a DOLLAR, to contain $375\frac{64}{100}$ grains of fine silver ; a HALF DOLLAR, to contain $187\frac{82}{100}$ grains of fine silver ; a DOUBLE DIME, to contain $75\frac{128}{1000}$ grains of fine silver ; a DIME, to contain $37\frac{560}{1000}$ grains of fine silver ; a CENT, of copper, equal to the 100th part of the federal dollar ; a HALF CENT, of the same metal, equal to the 200th part of the dollar.

But no mint had yet been established. It was not until the 16th of October, 1786, that congress passed " an ordinance for the establishment of a

Crown, of gold, value,...................	1,200	doits.
Half crown, " "	600	"
Dollar, of silver, "	300	"
Shilling, " "	100	"
Groat, " "	20	"
Doit, of copper, "	1	"

These coins were chosen for a double purpose, viz : their convenient size and their measures of weight, and of the values of the old currency. Each coin weighs an exact number of grains, without a fraction, and its value in this respect might thus be easily proved. Each one is an expression of an exact number of pence in the old currencies of the states, as well as in that of England, and in the livres and sous of France. They are all, moreover, decimal parts of the new unit, and thus adapted to the money of account."—*Sparks' Life of Gouverneur Morris.*

mint of the United States,[1] &c., the draft of which was reported by the Board of Treasury, agreeably to an order of August 8, 1786. The ordinance briefly designated the officers of the mint and their duties. It made no mention of devices; this matter and other details were probably committed to the Board of Treasury.

Meanwhile great quantities of base coppers were being circulated, which of course was highly injurious to trade and the commerce of the states. This bad currency consisted as well of the coppers manufactured by permission of the several states of the confederation, as of the great quantities daily imported. Congress therefore ordained that no foreign copper coins should be current within the United States of America after September 1, 1787, and that no copper coins struck under the authority of a particular state, should pass at a greater value than one federal dollar for $2\frac{1}{4}$ lbs. avoirdupois of such copper coin.

But though the several national coins had been specified and a mint directed to be organized, the project does not appear to have been fully carried out; for in 1787, the Board of Treasury reported several proposals from certain coin manufacturers for coining copper. These proposals were referred to a committee which subsequently reported in favor of that of Mr. James Jarvis. Congress thereupon authorized the Board to contract with Mr. Jarvis for 300 tons of copper coin of the federal standard—requir-

[1] See Appendix.

ing that it be coined at his own expense, but under
the inspection of an officer appointed and paid by the
United States ; that the obligations to be given for
the payment of the coin, be redeemable within
twenty years after the date of the contract. The
public copper on hand was to be disposed of either
by sale or contract for the coinage of the same. On
the 6th of July, 1787, it was ordered that the contractor for the copper coinage should stamp on one
side of each piece the following device, viz : Thirteen circles linked together, a small circle in the
middle, with the words UNITED STATES around it, and
in the center the words WE ARE ONE; on the other
side of the same piece the following device, viz: a
dial with the hours expressed on the face of it, a
meridian sun above, on one side of which the word
FUGIO, and on the other the year 1787; below the
dial the words MIND YOUR BUSINESS. (Pl. 3, fig. 7.)

Mr. Jarvis was one of the " Company for coining
coppers," in Connecticut; and as he was a share-
holder at the time the company ceased to manufacture coppers for that state, it is very probable that the coin above described was manufactured by him, at the Connecticut mint in New
Haven. Abel Buel, who had been previously associated with Mr. Jarvis, assisted him in its manufacture; he cut the dies, and indeed it is said that he
designed the same, which is not at all improbable,
judging from his conceded ingenuity. The coins
were struck at first in New Haven, but for how long
a time it is not known. Mr. Buel left the country

for Europe in 1788, having, previous to his depart-
ure, given to his son permission to coin coppers.
Wm. Buel fled[1] shortly after from New Haven to
Rupert in Vermont, where, in connection with Mr.
Harmon, he resumed the manufacture of the same
piece, at the mint used in the coinage of Vermont
coppers. He carried with him the original dies
used by his father at New Haven, and continued
the business of coining coppers until they had de-
preciated so much in value as to be worthless, or
nearly so, for circulation.

[1] Wm. Buel fled from New Haven under the following circumstances : Having had occasion to use some *aquafortis*, he procured a
quantity in a jug, from a druggist, and was returning to his residence when he was accosted by some Indians, who insisted upon
drinking from the jug what they assumed to be rum. He assured
them that he had no rum, and that what was contained in the jug
would poison them. But the Indians were not satisfied, and supposing this a mere excuse, seized the jug, and one of them took
a hearty swallow, which of course, at once produced his death. Mr.
Buel was accused of killing one of their number, and they, in accordance with their notions of justice, claimed his life, and watched
every opportunity to take it. But he evaded their vigilance by
leaving the country.

7

CHAPTER III.

COINS OF THE UNITED STATES, SINCE THE ADOPTION OF THE CONSTITUTION.

In September of the year 1787, congress received from the convention which framed the first constitution of the United States, the draft of that document. In accordance with a requirement therein contained, it was immediately submitted to the several states of the Union for their assent and approval. One article of the instrument provided that congress should have power to coin money, regulate the value thereof, and of foreign coins; and another, that no state should coin money, emit bills of credit, or make anything but gold and silver coin a tender in payment of debts. The constitution was ratified by eleven of the states, and was finally adopted by congress on the 13th of September, 1788.

The attention of the new congress, which began its first session on the 4th of March, 1789, was quite taken up in organizing the several departments of government, and in framing laws necessary to carry out the more immediate designs of the constitution.

Anticipating the action of congress in providing a currency for the country, a proposition was made by John H. Mitchell, a foreigner, to supply the United States with copper coinage " of any size and device, of pure unalloyed copper," for the sum of fourteen pence, sterling, the pound. He represented that his apparatus was such as to enable him to strike the edge at the same blow with the face. This invention, however, had before been brought to the notice of the congress of the confederation, by Mr. Jefferson, while he was residing in Paris. In a letter to Mr. Hopkinson dated Dec. 23, 1786, he writes: "a person here has invented a method of coining the French écu of six livres, so as to strike both faces and edge at one stroke."[1] He suggested that in case congress should establish a mint, one of the machines used in this process, and probably the services of Mr. Drost, the inventor, might be secured. Subsequent to the date of his letter to Mr. Hopkinson, he sent to John Jay specimens of this coinage, recommending very highly their perfection, and stating that from 25 to 30,000 pieces a day could be coined with the assistance of but two persons, the pieces of metal being first prepared.

The propositions of Mr. Mitchell were referred to the secretary of state (Mr. Jefferson), who for several reasons reported on them unfavorably.

1st. Because they supposed the pieces to be coined in a foreign country.

[1] Jefferson's Writings, vol. 2.

2d. Because transportation of the coins would expose them to acts of piracy.

3d. We would lose the opportunity of calling in and recoining the clipped money.

4th. We would lose the resource of coining up our household plate, in the instant of great distress.

5th. We would lose the means of forming artists to continue the works, when the common accidents of mortality should have deprived us of those who began them; and

Lastly. The carrying on of a coinage in a foreign country, so far as the secretary knew, was without example, and general example he considered weighty authority.

He therefore recommended that a mint when established, should be established at home. Other propositions for coining money in foreign parts were similarly disposed of.

Mr. Jefferson at once entered into a correspondence, with a view to ascertain whether the Swiss inventor, Drost, could be induced to come to this country with his implements, and be employed at the United States mint, if one should be established, or at all events, to come over and "erect the proper machinery, and instruct persons to go on with the coinage. An agreement was made, two coining mills or screws were ordered by him, but in the end he declined coming."[1]

Immediately after hearing the report of Mr. Jef-

[1] Jefferson's Writings.

ferson on the proposition of Mitchell, congress, on the 15th of April, 1790, instructed the secretary of the treasury to prepare and report a proper plan for the establishment of a national mint. To this important charge Alexander Hamilton gave a full and attentive consideration, and at the next session of congress presented an elaborate report thereon, discussing mainly the following points:

1st. What ought to be the nature of the money unit of the United States?

2d. What the proportion between gold and silver?

3d. What the proportion and composition of alloy in each kind?

4th. Whether the expense of coinage should be defrayed by the government or out of the material itself?

5th. What should be the number, denominations, sizes and devices of the coin?

6th. Whether foreign coins should be permitted to be current or not, at what rate, and for what period?

The resolution of the congress of the confederation, declaring the *dollar* to be the money unit of the United States, as well as that regulating the value of it, had never been practically carried out, so that it was difficult to say what our money unit really was. The pound was the unit of accounts, while the old Spanish piastres or "pieces of eight," with their various values, regulated our exchanges. It was on this account that it seemed most natural that the dollar, containing a specified exact amount

of pure silver, should be adopted as the unit in all
cases. But an objection suggested itself in the fact,
that the silver dollar had no standard value, while
gold had a fixed price, according to its fineness, and
Mr. Hamilton regarded the unit as having been hither-
to virtually attached to gold rather than to silver. He
therefore urged that the money unit should not be
attached to either gold or silver, because this could
not be done effectually without destroying the office
and character of one of them as money, and reducing
it to the situation of mere merchandise. Indeed it was
his idea that if either was preferred, it ought to be
gold rather than silver. His conclusions were, that
the unit might correspond with $24\frac{3}{4}$ grains of pure
gold, and with $371\frac{1}{4}$ grains of pure silver, each an-
swering to a dollar in the money of accounts. The
alloy in each case to be one-twelfth of the total
weight, which would make the unit 27 grains of
standard gold, and 405 grains of standard silver.
Each of these, it has been remarked, would answer
to a dollar in the money of account. Applying to
this the decimal subdivision as established Aug. 8,
1786, the unit in the money of account would continue to be a dollar, and its multiples, dimes, cents and
mills, or tenths, hundreds, thousands. He proposed
the following coins :

A gold piece (eagle), equal in weight and value
to ten units or dollars.

A gold piece (dollar), equal to a tenth part of the
former, and which shall be a unit or dollar.

A silver piece, which shall also be a unit or dollar.

A silver piece which shall be in weight and value, a tenth part of the silver unit or dollar.

A copper piece which shall be of the value of the hundredth part of the dollar.

A copper piece which shall be half the value of the former.[1]

Hamilton's report was transmitted to congress on the 28th of January, 1791. A concurrent resolution of the senate and house of representatives, passed on the 3d of March of the same year, declared that a mint should be established, and that the president should cause to be engaged such principal artists as should be necessary to carry out the resolutions, and also to procure such apparatus as should be requisite for the same purpose.[2]

The law "establishing a mint and regulating the coins of the United States," received the president's approval on the 2d of April, 1792. Its principal points were, the names of officers to be employed, viz: a director, an assayer, a chief coiner, an en-

1 It is not at all improbable that individuals who had implements of coinage experimented on some of the above named suggestions, in advance of any action at the mint.

2 Washington manifested a lively interest in the progress of this work, and frequently visited the mint. It is said that at one time he brought with him a quantity of silver bullion to be coined into half dimes, not for currency, but intended as presents for friends. Many patterns for gold, silver and copper coins were in this and ensuing year, prepared and submitted for approval. Especially curious and interesting among these are the specimens for cents, a number of which, including those known as Washington cents, are described in the concluding chapter of this work.

graver, a treasurer,[1] the names of the coins to be struck, viz : EAGLES, each to be of the value of ten dollars or units, and to contain $247\frac{4}{8}$ grains of pure, or 270 grains of standard gold; HALF EAGLES, each to be of the value of five dollars, and to contain $123\frac{6}{8}$ grains of pure, or 135 grains of standard gold; QUARTER EAGLES, each to be of the value of $2\frac{1}{2}$ dollars, and to contain $61\frac{7}{8}$ grains of pure, or $67\frac{4}{8}$ grains of standard gold;[2] DOLLARS or UNITS, each to be of the value of a Spanish milled dollar as the same is now current, and to contain $371\frac{4}{16}$ grains of pure, or 416 grains of standard silver; HALF DOLLARS, each to be half the value of the dollar or unit, and to contain $185\frac{10}{16}$ grains of pure, or 208 grains of standard silver; QUARTER DOLLARS, each to be of one-fourth the value of the dollar or unit, and to contain $92\frac{13}{16}$ grains of pure, or 104 grains of standard silver; DISMES, each to be of the value of one-tenth of a dollar or unit, and to contain $37\frac{2}{16}$ grains of pure, or $41\frac{3}{5}$ grains of standard silver; HALF DISMES, each to be of the value of one-twentieth of a dollar, and to contain $18\frac{9}{16}$ grains of pure, or $20\frac{4}{5}$ grains of

[1] The office of melter and refiner was created by the act of 1837.

[2] DOUBLE EAGLES, of the value of twenty dollars, and GOLD DOLLARS, of the value of one dollar or unit, were authorized by a law passed in 1849. These were directed to be struck and coined, conformably in all respects to law (except that on the reverse of the gold dollar the figure of the eagle should be omitted), and conformably in all respects to the standard of gold coins then established. THREE DOLLAR gold coins were coined under similar regulations, under an act passed in 1853, except that the devices and shape of the same should be fixed by the secretary of the treasury.

standard silver;[1] CENTS, each to be of the value of the
one-hundredth part of a dollar, and to contain eleven
pennyweights of copper;[2] [3] HALF CENTS, each to be
of the value of half a cent, and to contain $5\frac{1}{2}$ pwts.
of copper.[4]

[1] By a law passed in 1851, a piece of the denomination and value
of THREE CENTS, (a) to be composed of three-fourths silver and one-
fourth copper, and to weigh 12 3-8 grains, (b) was authorized. The
devices were to be conspicuously different from those of the other
silver coins and of the gold dollar, but having the inscription
"United States of America," and its denomination and date.

[2] Jan. 26, 1796, President Washington issued a proclamation, that
"on account of the increased price of copper and the expense of
coinage," the cent would be reduced to 7 doits or 168 grains, and
the half cent in proportion.

[3] "The standard weight of the CENT coined at the mint shall be
seventy-two grains, or three-twentieths of one ounce troy, with no
greater deviation than four grains in each piece; the said cent shall
be composed of 88 per centum of copper and 12 per centum of
nickel, and of such shape and device as may be fixed by the secretary of the treasury; and the coinage of the HALF CENT shall
cease."—*Act of* 1857.

[4] The contents of these several pieces have been altered by subsequent laws, viz: In 1837—"The weight of the Eagle shall be 258
grains; that of the Half Eagle 129 grains; and that of the Quarter
Eagle $64\frac{1}{2}$ grains." "Of the silver coins, the Dollar shall be of the
weight of $412\frac{1}{2}$ grains." In 1853—"The weight of the Half Dollar
or piece of fifty cents, shall be 192 grains; and the Quarter Dollar,
Dime and Half Dime, shall be respectively, one-half, one-fifth and
one-tenth of the weight of said Half-Dollar."

(a) As early as 1807, Jefferson suggested that silver pieces of the value of two
and three cents, and gold dollars, should be coined.

(b) Law of 1853: "Hereafter the Three Cent coin now authorized by law, shall
be of the weight of three-fiftieths of the weight of the half dollar, and of the same
standard of fineness."

The devices and legends to be stamped on the coins were prescribed also, by law, and were as follows: Upon one side an impression emblematical of liberty,[1] with an inscription of the word LIBERTY, and the year of the coinage; upon the reverse of the gold and silver coins a figure or representation of an eagle,[2] with the inscription UNITED STATES OF AMERICA;[3] and upon the reverse of the copper coins, an inscription which should express the denomination of the piece. The standard for gold coins was fixed at 11 parts fine to 1 part alloy; for silver 1485 parts fine and 179 parts alloy.[4]

[1] The words "emblematical of liberty, with an inscription of the word LIBERTY," were substituted in the house of representatives, for the following, which had been adopted by the senate, viz: *a representation of the head of the president which shall express the initial or first letter of his Christian or first name, and his surname at length, the succession of the presidency numerically.* The senate at first refused to adopt the amendment, but the house of representatives persisting, the senate receded.—*Journal of H. of R.*, 1791-2.

[2] "But on the reverse of the Dime and Half Dime, Cent and Half Cent the figure of the eagle shall be omitted."—*Act of* 1837. The figure of the eagle was also omitted on the reverse of the Three Dollar, One Dollar, and Three-Cent pieces.

[3] The latin motto "E Pluribus Unum," floated in a scroll over the eagle's head, until the change of standard in 1837, when it was discontinued.—*Eckfeldt and Du Bois.*

[4] "The standard for both gold and silver coins shall hereafter be such, that of 1000 parts by weight, nine hundred shall be of pure metal and one hundred of alloy; and the alloy of the silver coins shall be of copper, and the alloy of the gold coins shall be of copper and silver: provided that the silver does not exceed one-half of the whole alloy."—*Act of* 1837.

President Washington proceeded at once to carry out the intentions of the act, and as Philadelphia was then the seat of government, he there caused the necessary buildings and machinery to be provided and put in a condition for the purposes of coining; and in the fall of the same year that the mint act was passed, he informed congress that a small beginning had been made in the coinage of half dollars[1] and cents. The offices of artist, chief coiner and assayer, were of course, considered of great importance, and it was the intention to employ those who were most skilled in these professions; and as these arts had been but little practiced in our own country, efforts were made to procure artisans from abroad. Mr. Jefferson again endeavored to secure the services of Drost, but not being successful, Mr. Pinckney, who was then our minister at London, engaged Mr. Albion Coxe, as assayer. Henry Voight, an artist of the United States, performed the duties of the office of chief coiner, and also for a considerable length of time made the dies.

Copper coinage at the mint may be said to have

[1] A few half dollars bearing this date are extant. They have on the obverse, a bust of Washington in military costume; legend, G. WASHINGTON, PRESIDENT I, 1792 : reverse, a spread eagle, holding in one talon a bundle of thirteen arrows, and in the other an olive branch ; legend, UNITED STATES OF AMERICA. The die of this piece is said to have been made by an engraver in Lancaster, Pa., named Gætz, by way of recommendation for the office of engraver in the mint, to which, however, he was not appointed.

been fairly commenced in 1793; silver was coined first in the latter part of 1794, and gold in the summer of 1795. In 1794, the director of the mint reported that nearly one million of cents had been coined. Many difficulties, however, attended the early minting operations. The establishment was more extensive than any which had heretofore been erected in this country, and experiments had to be made at almost every step in its progress; workmen who had been engaged in Europe often failed to come, and others were not masters of their business. Materials for the machinery were with difficulty procured, even the tools necessary to make the machinery and implements were first to be made, and both were manufactured at the mint; the latter were prepared chiefly under the direction of Mr. Voight. The construction of the mint was mainly upon theory, which of course, created greater delay and expense than full, practical knowledge would have found necessary. The cost of building, apparatus and machinery up to February 1795, was $22,720. Up to that date there were three presses, one of which would coin 10,000 cents a day; the machinery was moved by horse power.

The expectations of the public were not realized as regarded the economy in conducting, or in the relief the mint afforded to the now diminished copper circulation of the country. The expense or charge on the nation for its maintenance was considerable, and naturally from year to year increased rather than diminished. An opinion generally prevailed, that the establishment was unnecessarily expensive, and in fact " less productive than was rationally expected by its advocates and friends." There was some foundation for this complaint. One of the principles of the act establishing the mint was, that the whole coinage, including refining, was to be executed at the public expense, the depositor being fully indemnified.[1] The person who brought bullion in its debased state to the mint, received as much coin for the standard metal contained therein, as he whose bullion had been previously refined, so that the expense of assaying and refining was a public charge. Again, the mint had no means of purchasing bullion. Every deposit of metal had to be coined as soon as possible, in order that the depositor might not lose the benefit of the use of the coin; therefore the clippings and grains of each deposit were necessarily on each occasion of deposit, melted. With the means on hand of payment at once of the amount due on deposits, the coinage of such deposits might have been more conveniently and more economically carried on. The small deposits would then have been kept in the vaults until a large amount

[1] " The only subjects of charge of the mint to the depositor shall be the following : for refining when the bullion is below standard; for toughening, when metals are contained in it which render it unfit for coinage; for copper used for alloy when the bullion is above standard ; for silver introduced into the alloy of gold; and for separating the gold and silver when these metals exist together in the bullion."—*Act of* 1837.

had accumulated, and then coined, as the expense of coining a small quantity of bullion was nearly as great as that of an amount many times larger.

Many of the leading men of the country began to doubt the propriety of continuing a government establishment which, as they contended, cost more than the benefits derived from it; and there was an opinion that the bank of the United States could coin for the nation at a less expense, or that the work could be done by contract.[1]

Mr. Giles, accordingly, in the house of representatives on the 29th of January, 1802, submitted a resolution, declaring that the several acts in relation to the mint ought to be repealed. This he presented not as pressing the repeal of the laws, but with a view to discover the opinions of the house on the subject. In the debate, however, he stated that he was for abolishing the institution altogether, as he could see no propriety in continuing it. The discussion on the subject was general and earnest, and the resolution finally passed the house. In the senate it was promptly negatived, and thus the matter was put to rest for that session.

It was early taken up in the fall of 1802, by John Randolph, and repeal was strenuously urged on arguments not unlike those advanced at the previous session. The senate, it was quite well understood,

[1] Propositions had been already made to the secretary of the treasury, to undertake to supply the coins of the United States in case the mint should be abolished.

would not sanction the repeal, and as the act establishing the mint would expire by limitation on the next 4th of March, if reënacted, new and more ample accommodations would be required. The lots then occupied were too small; both the machinery and the horses were worn out, (!) and it would be necessary that steam power should be provided. The property of the mint at that time was indeed meagre. All told, it was comprised in the following schedule, viz:

Two lots on 7th street, between Market and Arch streets, with a dwelling house on the north lot, and a shell of a house and a stable on the south lot.

A lot on Sugar alley.

A frame building, improved for a large furnace, in the commons at the north end of 6th street.

Copper planchettes, about 22 tons.

Three horses, good for little but for the use of the mint.

Five striking presses, with machinery.

Three cutting presses.

One milling machine.

Five pair of rollers—great and small.

One drawing machine.

Three pair of smith's bellows.

A set of blacksmith's tools.

A large number of hubs and dies.

Carpenters' tools.

Seven stoves.

One turning lathe.

Six scale beams, scales and weights.

Two sets assay scales, and sundry adjusting scales

Furniture in the clerk's room.

Various implements used in the several departments.

About 2000 bushels of charcoal.

Engravers' tools, pots, bottles, &c., an old horse,
cart and gears.

About 2000 fire brick; a considerable quantity of
old iron.

The director of the mint thought that the horses
might last another year.[1]

Considering this condition of affairs, the house of
representatives adopted a resolution directing inquiry as to the amount the whole property of the
mint would probably sell for, and the expense of
more suitable buildings, machinery, &c. At the
same session, a law was passed continuing the act
of 1792 for five years, which was repeatedly renewed
until 1828, when it was enacted, that the act of
March 3, 1801, should remain in force and operation
until otherwise provided by law.[2]

Branches of the mint of the United States were
established in 1835 at the city of New Orleans, for
the coinage of silver and gold, and at the town of
Charlotte in Mecklinburg county, N. C., and at or
near Dahlonega in Lumpkin county, Ga., for the

[1] American State Papers—Finance, v. 1.

[2] This act directed that the mint should remain in Philadelphia,
until March 4, 1803.

coinage of gold only ; in 1852 in California, for the coinage of gold and silver. By an act passed in 1853, an office for the receipt, and for the melting, refining, parting and assaying of gold and silver bullion and foreign coin, and for casting the same into bars, &c., was established at New York.

The director of the mint at Philadelphia, subordinate to the secretary of the treasury, has supervisory powers over these establishments, and the laws of the United States for the government of the mint and its officers, as far as the same are applicable, are extended to them. The assistant treasurer of the United States, in New York, is the treasurer of the assay office.

TABULAR STATEMENT

OF THE AMOUNT OF COINAGE AT THE MINT OF THE UNITED STATES SINCE THE COMMENCEMENT OF ITS OPERATIONS.

NOTE.—The regular emission of Copper from the Mint was commenced in 1793; that of Silver in 1794. The exact amount of the respective coins struck during these years, is not known.

GOLD COINAGE.

Period.	Double Eagles. PIECES.	Eagles. PIECES.	Half Eagles. PIECES.	Three Dollars. PIECES.	Quarter Eagles. PIECES.	Dollars. PIECES.
1795		2,795	8,707			
1796		6,934	6,196		963	
1797		8,323	3,609		859	
1798		7,974	24,867		614	
1799		17,483	7,451		480	
1800		25,965	11,622			
1801		29,254	26,006			
1802		15,090	53,176		2,612	
1803		8,979	33,506		423	
1804		9,795	30,475		3,327	
1805			33,183		1,781	
1806			64,093		1,616	
1807			84,093		6,812	
1808			55,578		2,710	
1809			33,875			

Year				
1810			100,287	
1811			99,581	
1812			58,087	
1813			95,428	
1814			15,454	
1815	6,448		635	
1816				
1817				
1818			48,588	
1819			51,723	
1820	2,600		263,806	
1821	4,434		34,641	
1822	760		17,796	
1823	2,800		14,485	
1824			17,340	
1825	3,403		29,060	
1826	4,540		18,069	
1827	4,520		24,913	
1828	4,400		28,029	
1829	4,160		57,442	
1830	117,370		126,351	
1831	131,402		140,594	
1832	547,986		157,487	
1833	45,080		193,630	
1834	47,030		732,169	
1835	27,021		371,534	
1836			553,147	
1837			207,121	
1838		7,200	286,588	
1839		38,248	118,143	

Period	Double Eagles. PIECES.	Eagles. PIECES.	Half Eagles. PIECES.	Three Dollars. PIECES.	Quarter Eagles. PIECES.	Dollars. PIECES.
1840		47,338	137,382		18,859	
1841		63,131	15,833			
1842		81,507	27,578		2,823	
1843		250,624	855,085		530,853	
1844		125,061	817,583		35,738	
1845		73,653	548,728		110,511	
1846		101,875	547,231		111,709	
1847		1,433,764	1,080,337		192,824	
1848		145,484	260,775		8,886	
1849		653,618	133,070		23,294	688,567
1850	1,170,261	291,451	64,491		252,923	481,953
1851	2,087,155	176,328	377,505		1,372,748	3,317,671
1852	2,053,026	263,106	573,901		1,159,681	2,045,351
1853	1,261,326	201,253	305,770		1,404,668	4,076,051
1854	757,899	54,250	160,675	138,618	596,258	1,639,445
1855	364,666	121,701	117,098	50,555	235,480	758,269
	7,694,333	3,267,542	9,197,040	189,173	6,301,564	13,007,307

SILVER COINAGE.

Period.	Dollars. PIECES.	Half Dollars. PIECES.	Quarter Dol'rs. PIECES.	Dimes. PIECES.	Half Dimes. PIECES.	Three Cents. PIECES.
1795	204,791	323,144	......	......	86,416	
1796	72,920	3,918	5,894	22,135	10,230	
1797	7,746	......	252	25,261	44,527	
1798	327,536	......	......	27,550	......	
1799	423,515	......	......	......	......	
1800	220,920	30,289	......	21,760	24,000	
1801	54,454	29,890	......	34,640	33,910	
1802	41,650	31,715	......	10,975	13,010	
1803	66,064	156,519	6,738	33,040	37,850	
1804	19,570	211,722	121,394	8,265	......	
1805	321	211,722	121,394	120,780	15,600	
1806	......	1,051,576	206,124	......		
1807	......	839,576	220,643	165,000		
1808	......	1,368,600	......	......		
1809	......	1,405,810	......	44,710		
1810	......	1,276,276	......	6,355		
1811	......	1,203,644	......	65,180		
1812	......	1,628,059	......	......		
1813	......	1,241,903	......	......		
1814	......	1,039,075	......	421,500		
1815	......	......	69,232	......		
1816	......	47,150	20,003	......		

Period.	Dollars. PIECES.	Half Dollars. PIECES.	Quarter Dol'rs. PIECES.	Dimes. PIECES.	Half Dimes. PIECES.	Three Cents. PIECES.
1817	....	1,215,567	....	....	....	
1818	....	1,960,322	361,174	....	....	
1819	....	2,208,000	144,000	....	....	
1820	....	751,122	127,444	942,587	....	
1821	....	1,305,797	216,851	1,186,512	....	
1822	....	1,559,573	64,080	100,000	....	
1823	....	1,694,200	17,800	440,000	....	
1824	....	3,504,954	*		....	
1825	....	2,943,166	168,000	510,000	....	
1826	....	1,004,180			....	
1827	....	5,493,400	4,000	1,215,000	....	
1828	....	3,075,200	102,000	125,000	....	
1829	....	3,712,156	.....	770,000	1,230,000	
1830	....	4,764,800	.....	510,000	1,240,000	
1831	....	5,873,660	398,000	771,350	1,242,700	
1832	....	4,797,000	320,000	522,500	965,000	
1833	....	5,206,000	156,000	485,000	1,370,000	
1834	....	6,412,004	286,000	635,000	1,480,000	
1835	....	5,352,006	1,952,000	1,410,000	2,760,000	
1836	1,000	6,546,200	472,000	1,190,000	1,900,000	
1837	....	3,629,820	252,400	1,042,000	2,276,000	
1838	....	3,546,000	832,000	1,992,500	2,255,000	
1839	300	3,334,561	491,146	1,053,115	1,069,150	
1840	61,005	1,435,008	188,127	1,358,580	1,344,085	

1841	173,000	310,000	120,000	1,622,500	1,150,000	
1842	184,618	2,012,764	88,000	1,887,500	815,000	
1843	165,100	6,112,000	1,613,600	1,520,000	1,165,000	
1844	20,000	3,771,000	1,161,200	72,500	650,000	
1845	24,500	2,683,000	922,000	1,985,000	1,564,000	
1846	169,600	4,514,000	510,000	31,300	27,000	
1847	140,750	3,740,000	1,102,000	245,000	1,274,000	
1848	15,000	580,000	146,000	451,500	668,000	
1849	62,600	1,252,000	340,000	839,000	1,309,000	
1850	7,500	227,000	190,800	1,931,500	955,000	
1851	1,300	200,750	160,000	1,026,500	781,000	5,477,400
1852	1,100	77,130	177,060	1,535,500	1,000,500	18,663,500
1853	46,110	3,532,708	15,254,220	12,173,010	13,345,020	11,400,000
1854	33,140	2,982,000	12,380,000	4,470,000	5,740,000	671,000
1855	26,000	759,500	2,857,000	2,075,000	1,750,000	139,000
	2,513,140	117,712,414	42,149,182	48,752,105	51,370,998	36,325,900

* A small amount struck—no record kept.

Period.	COPPER COINAGE.*		RECAPITULATION.	
	Cents. PIECES.	Half Cents. PIECES.	Whole Coinage in Pieces.	Whole Coinage in Value.
1795.....	1,066,033	142,534	1,834,420	$453,541·80
1796.....	974,700	115,480	1,219,370	192,129·40
1797.....	897,510	107,048	1,095,165	125,524·29
1798.....	979,700	....	1,368,241	545,698·00
1799.....	904,585	12,167	1,365,681	645,907·68
1800.....	2,822,175	211,530	3,337,972	571,335·40
1801.....	1,362,837	....	1,571,390	510,956·37
1802.....	3,435,100	14,366	3,615,869	516,075·83
1803.....	2,471,353	97,900	2,780,830	370,698·53
1804.....	756,838	1,055,312	2,046,839	371,827·94
1805.....	941,116	814,464	2,260,361	333,239·48
1806.....	348,000	356,000	1,815,409	801,084·00
1807.....	727,221	476,000	2,731,345	1,044,595·96
1808.....	1,109,000	400,000	2,935,888	982,055·00
1809.....	222,867	1,154,572	2,861,834	884,752·53
1810.....	2,458,500	215,000	3,056,418	1,155,868·50
1811.....	218,025	63,140	1,649,570	1,108,740·95
1812.....	1,075,500	....	2,761,646	1,115,219·50
1813.....	418,000	†	1,755,331	1,102,271·50
1814.....	357,830	....	1,833,859	642,535·80
1815.....	....	....	69,867	20,483·00
1816.....	2,820,982	....	2,888,135	56,785·57
1817.....	3,948,400	....	5,163,967	647,267·50
1818.....	3,167,000	....	5,537,084	1,345,064·50
1819.....	2,671,000	....	5,074,723	1,425,325·00
1820.....	4,407,550	....	6,492,509	1,864,786·20
1821.....	389,000	....	3,139,249	1,018,977·45
1822.....	2,072,339	....	3,813,788	915,509·89
1823.....	†	....	2,166,485	967,975·00
1824.....	1,262,000	....	4,786,894	1,858,297·00
1825.....	1,461,100	63,000	5,178,760	1,735,894·00
1826.....	1,517,425	234,000	5,774,434	2,110,679·25
1827.....	2,357,732	....	9,097,845	3,024,342·32
1828.....	2,260,624	606,000	6,196,853	1,741,381·24
1829.....	1,414,500	487,000	7,674,501	2,306,875·50
1830.....	1,711,500	....	8,357,191	3,155,620·00
1831.....	3,359,260	2,200	11,792,284	3,923,473·60
1832.....	2,362,000	†	9,128,387	3,401,055·00
1833.....	2,739,000	154,000	10,307,790	3,765,710·00

* See note, page 66.   † A small amount struck—no record kept.

Period.	COPPER COINAGE.		RECAPITULATION.	
	Cents. PIECES.	Half Cents. PIECES.	Whole Coinage in Pieces.	Whole Coinage in Value.
1834.....	1,855,100	120,000	11,637,643	7,388,423·00
1835.....	3,878,400	141,000	15,996,342	5,668,667·00
1836.....	2,111,000	398,000	13,719,333	7,764,900·00
1837.....	5,558,300	....	13,010,721	3,299,898·00
1838.....	6,370,200	....	15,780,311	4,206,540·00
1839.....	3,128,661	....	11,811,594	3,576,467·61
1840.....	2,462,700	....	10,558,240	3,426,632·50
1841.....	1,597,367	....	8,811,968	2,240,321·17
1842.....	2,383,390	....	11,743,153	4,190,754·40
1843.....	2,428,320	....	14,640,582	11,967,830·70
1844.....	2,398,752	....	9,051,834	7,687,767·52
1845.....	3,894,804	....	11,806,196	5,668,595·54
1846.....	4,120,800	....	10,133,515	6,633,965·50
1847.....	6,183,669	....	15,392,344	22,657,671·69
1848.....	6,415,799	....	8,691,444	3,265,137·99
1849.....	4,178,500	39,864	9,519,513	8,913,266·32
1850.....	4,426,844	39,812	10,039,535	28,210,513·00
1851.....	9,889,707	147,672	24,985,736	52,689,878·43
1852.....	5,063,094	....	32,611,949	52,403,679·44
1853.....	6,641,131	129,694	69,775,537	60,111,249·72
1854.....	4,236,156	55,358	33,919,921	43,108,977·93
1855.....	1,574,829	56,500	10,885,619	12,045,952·93
	153,264,825	7,909,613	499,659,853	$377,383,808·87

10

CHAPTER IV.

MISCELLANEOUS COINAGE.

Concerning a large number of pieces which circulated in America during the early years of the republic, and which were manufactured from time to time without the authority or sanction of law; including also many which are known to have been struck only as patterns, or specimens of coinage, of which character are a large proportion of those hereinafter mentioned, simply a brief enumeration and short description of each, will suffice for the purposes of this work. For obvious reasons therefore, no mention will be made of a large number of tradesmen's, political and Washington tokens, nor of certain private issues of recent dates.

The specimens can be readily referred to by observing the chronological arrangement.

1737   At Granby, Conn., about the year 1737, coppers circulated, called Highley's coppers. They were manufactured by Dr. Samuel Highley (said to have been an eccentric genius), who carried on this business clandestinely, without any authority from the colony. The manufacturing establishment was but an ordinary sized shop, situated in the vicinity of the copper mines,[1] near which he resided. He continued the business only a few years, and the number of coppers struck was not large, their circulation being limited to a small number of towns, in the vicinity. They bore the following devices, &c. : On one side, a deer ; legend, VALVE ME AS YOU PLEASE, and a star: on the opposite side, three hammers, each surmounted by a crown; legend, I AM GOOD COPPER, 1737. Another variety had on the opposite side, a broad axe ; legend, I CUT MY WAY THROUGH. They are said to have passed for two and sixpence, in paper currency, it is presumed.[2] (Pl. 3, fig. 1.)

1776 A copper piece, nearly the size of a half dollar. Obverse, a pine tree; legend, MASSACHUSETTS STATE: reverse, a female seated on a globe, holding in her right hand an olive leaf, and in her left a staff; legend, LIBERTY and VIRTUE, 1776.

1776 A copper piece, size of a half cent ; on one side a Janus head: reverse, GODESS OF LIBERTY, 1776.[3]

1776 A piece, copies of which are occasionally found in white metal, was struck in 1776. It is an inch and

[1] For an account of these mines, see History of Simsbury, Granby and Canton, by Noah A. Phelps.

[2] Phelps's Hist. of Granby copper mines.

[3] A writer in the *Historical Magazine*, attributes the dies of the last two specimens to Col. Paul Revere, of Boston, who was by trade a goldsmith and engraver. A short account of him is given in *Lossing's Field Book*, vol. 1, p. 317.

a half in diameter. Obverse, a dial, and the motto
MIND YOUR BUSINESS,[1] beneath; legend, CONTINENTAL
CURENCY, 1776, and in another ring within, a meridian sun, with the word FUGIO: reverse, a circle
formed by thirteen small rings, with the names of
the states inscribed on them; on a ring within this
circle, AMERICAN CONGRESS, and in the center, WE
ARE ONE. In another variety of the same coin, one
letter R is added in the word "currency," and "Eg
fecit" is added in the inner circle. On the reverse,
Amer[n] Congress, instead of "American Congress."
There is no reference to these pieces in the journals
of congress, but the description corresponds very
nearly with that ordered by congress in 1787. Bishop
Watson must be in error in supposing the American
congress issued it.[2]

1778   A copper piece, size of a cent. Obverse, a bust;
legend, NON. DEPEN–DENS STATUS: reverse, a full
length figure of an Indian seated on a globe, with a
girdle about his loins. In his right hand, which is
extended, he holds a branch of tobacco; his left
hand rests on a shield, on which is the American
flag and sword, crossed, and the *fleur de lis* of France;
legend, AMERICA. Exergue, 1778.[3]

1783   A copper piece, size of a cent. Obverse, an eye,

---

[1] Probably a suggestion of Franklin. See Diplomatic Correspondence of the American Revolution, vol. 3, p. 107, and Franklin's
works, v. 8, page 384.

[2] See Chemical Essays, vol. 4, p. 136.

[3] See Norton's Literary Letter, No. 2.

with rays diverging from it, around which is a circle of thirteen stars ; legend, NOVA CONSTELLATIO : reverse, a wreath, encircling the letters U. S.; legend, LIBERTAS ET JUSTITIA. 1783. There are several varieties of this piece. They were frequently struck over other coppers.

1783   A brass piece, size of a cent. Obverse, a laureated head; legend, WASHINGTON & INDEPENDENCE, 1783 : reverse, a wreath, within which the words ONE CENT; legend, UNITY STATES OF AMERICA. Exergue, $\frac{1}{100}$.

1783   A copper piece, size of a cent. Obverse, same as the last : reverse, a figure of Liberty seated, in her right hand an olive branch, and in her left a staff, surmounted by a liberty cap; legend, UNITED STATES.

1783   A copper piece, size of a cent. Obverse, a bust in military costume; legend, WASHINGTON & INDEPENDENCE, 1783 : reverse, same as the last.

1783   J. Chalmers, a silversmith or watchmaker, of Annapolis, Md., issued money in 1783. The pieces bearing his name, consist of a shilling, six pence and three pence ; the former equal in value to the Maryland state currency, and the six pence and three pence proportionably valued. The undertaking proved unprofitable to him, and he shortly discontinued it. The obverse side of the shilling bore a wreath, encircling two clasped hands ; legend, I. CHALMERS, ANNAPOLIS: reverse, a figure of a serpent, and beneath, two birds with a branch in their beaks; legend, 8 ONE SHILLING, 8, 1783. (Pl. 2, fig. 6.)

1785   A copper piece, size of a cent. Obverse, an eye, with rays diverging from it, around which a circle

of thirteen stars; legend, NOVA CONSTELLATIO : reverse, a wreath encircling the letters (in scrip) U
S; legend, LIBERTAS ET JUSTITIA. 1785.

1785   A copper piece, size of a cent. Obverse, an Indian
standing beside a pedestal, his right foot resting on
a crown, an arrow in his right hand, a bow in his
left and a quiver on his back; legend, INIMICA TY-
RANNIS AMERICANA: reverse, a constellation of thirteen stars, with rays diverging; legend, CONFEDERA-
TIO, 1785.

1785   A gold piece, size of a cent.   Obverse, a female
seated on a box of merchandise, her right hand extended and suspending a pair of scales, in her left a
staff with a flag partially unfurled, and a liberty cap
at the top; legend, IMMUNE COLUMBIA, exergue, 1785:
reverse, an eye, with rays diverging, and surrounded
by thirteen stars; legend, NOVA CONSTELLATIO.

1785   A silver piece, same as last.

1786   A copper piece, size of a cent. Obverse, the letters
U. S. A., the S. which is larger than the other letters,
extends partially across them : reverse, thirteen
bars, parallel to each other.   There is barely a pro-
bability that this piece was struck in 1786.

1786   The same, reduced to the size of a half cent.

1786   A copper piece, size of a cent.   Obverse, a female
figure seated, her right hand extended and suspending a pair of scales; in her left a staff with a flag
partially unfurled, and surmounted with a liberty
cap; legend, IMMUNIS COLUMBIA, exergue, 1786 : reverse, a shield, same as on the New Jersey cent;

legend, E PLURIBUS UNUM. A pattern supposed to
have been struck by Col. Reed, of Uxbridge.

1786 A copper piece, size of a cent. Obverse, a bust
facing the right, probably intended for Washington;
legend, NON VI VIRTUTE VICI: reverse, a female figure
seated, facing the right, in her right hand a staff
surmounted by a liberty cap, her left hand extended
and holding a pair of scales; legend, NEO–EBORACEN-
SIS. Exergue, 1786. (Pl. 4, fig. 3.)

1787 A copper piece, size of a cent. Obverse, a bust,
facing the right, in Roman armour, with a laurel
wreath; legend, * NOVA * EBORAC *: reverse, a
female figure seated, facing the left, holding in her
right hand a sprig of laurel, and in her left a staff
surmounted by a cap of liberty, at her side a shield
with the arms of the state; legend, * VIRT. ET. LIB. *.
Exergue, 1787. (Pl. 4, fig. 1.)

1787 A copper piece, size of a cent. Obverse, an Indian
chief, with a tomahawk in his right hand and a bow
in his left, a quiver with arrows on his back; legend,
LIBER NATUS LIBERTATEM DEFENDO*: reverse, the
arms of the state of New York; legend, EXCELSIOR.
Exergue, 1787. (Pl. 4, fig. 2.)

1787 A copper piece, size of a cent. Obverse, same as
the last: reverse, an eagle proper on a half globe;
legend, NEO EBORACUS, 1787, EXCELSIOR. (Pl. 4, fig. 4.)

The four specimens last described, are commonly
called the New York tokens, and were struck, of
course, without the authority of law. No enactment
in relation to coinage was ever made by the state of

New York. The action of neighboring states, as well as petitioners praying for the privilege of coining money, frequently suggested the subject to the legislature. John Bailey and Ephraim Brasher, in 1787 petitioned the assembly in relation to the manufacture of coppers. The matter was referred to a committee, with instructions to bring in a bill to regulate the circulation of copper coins within the state. This committee being at a loss to determine the extent of the intended regulation, whether it was only to ascertain the value of pieces then in circulation, or was to extend to a new coinage, presented to the house the result of their inquiries on the subject. The proposition to contract with parties for a supply of coinage, was generally regarded as a matter of mere speculation, and this idea having been strengthened by the statements of the investigations made by the committee, the further consideration of the matter was postponed.

1787   A copper piece, size of a cent. Obverse, a bust of Gov. George Clinton, facing the right; legend, GEORGE * CLINTON: reverse, the arms of the state of New York; legend, EXCELSIOR. Exergue, 1787.

1787   A copper piece, size of a cent. Obverse, a laureated head; legend, AUCTORI PLEBIS: reverse, a female seated, a globe at her right hand, and at her left an anchor, on which she leans; legend, INDEP. ET LIBER. Exergue, 1787.

1787   A copper piece, size of a cent. Obverse, a female figure seated on a globe, her right hand extended and suspending a pair of scales, in her left a staff with a flag partially unfurled, and surmounted with a liberty cap; legend, IMMUNIS COLUMBIA; exergue, 1787: reverse, an eagle, spread, with thirteen arrows in the left talon and an olive branch in the other; legend, E * PLURIBUS * UNUM *. A pattern supposed to have been struck by Col. Reed, of Uxbridge.

1787   A gold piece, size of a cent. Obverse, the arms of the state of New York as found on the great seal of 1777, viz: the sun rising from behind the hills, with a representation of the sea in front; on a scroll beneath, *Brasher;* legend, NOVA EBORACA. COLUMBIA. EXCELSIOR: reverse, a wreath encircling a spread eagle, holding in its right talon a bunch of thirteen arrows, and in its left an olive branch; legend, UNUM E PLURIBUS. 1787. It was struck in New York, by Ephraim Brasher, a goldsmith, whose place of business was No. 1 Cherry street.

1791   A copper piece, rather larger than a cent. Obverse, a bust of Washington, with military costume; legend, WASHINGTON, PRESIDENT, 1791: reverse, a spread eagle, large, holding in its right talon thirteen arrows, and in its left an olive branch; from its beak a scroll, inscribed Unum E Pluribus; above the eagle's head ONE CENT; on the edge, UNITED STATES OF AMERICA.

1791   A copper piece, rather larger than a cent. Obverse, same as the last, only the date is omitted: reverse, a spread eagle, small, holding in its right talon six arrows, and in its left an olive branch;

11

clouds above the eagle's head and eight stars. At
the top of the piece, ONE CENT, and at the bottom,
1791; on the edge, UNITED STATES OF AMERICA.

1791   A copper piece, size of a cent. Obverse, a hand
holding a scroll partially unrolled, and upon which
is inscribed OUR CAUSE IS JUST; legend, UNANIMITY
IS THE STRENGTH OF SOCIETY : reverse, a triangle of
fifteen stars, with rays diverging from the outer
ones, on the stars are engraved the initial letters of
fifteen states; legend, E PLURIBUS UNUM. It was
struck in Lancaster, Eng., in 1791, and is called the
Kentucky cent, from the fact, that the star designated K., for Kentucky, is placed at the top of the
triangle. (Pl. 2, fig. 8.)

1791   The same, in silver.

1792   A copper piece, size of a half dollar. Obverse, a
bust of a female figure, with flowing hair, facing the
right, beneath the bust, 1792; legend, LIBERTY PA-
RENT OF SCIENCE & INDUSTRY: reverse, a wreath
encircling a circle, and the words ONE CENT; legend,
UNITED STATES OF AMERICA. Exergue, $\frac{1}{100}$. There
are half cents of this date.

1792   A copper piece, about the size of a ten cent coin.
Obverse and reverse the same as the last described
piece, except that the bust faces the left, and in the
center of the piece is inserted a small piece of silver.

1792   A silver piece, size of a dime. Obverse, a bust of
Liberty, flowing hair, facing the left; legend, LIB.
PAR. OF SCIENCE & INDUSTRY; beneath the bust
1792 : reverse, a flying eagle; legend, UNI. STATES OF

AMERICA across the field; beneath the eagle, HALF DISME; below, a star.

1792 A copper piece, larger than a dime. Obverse, same as the last; legend, LIBERTY PARENT OF SCIENCE & INDUSTRY: reverse, a flying eagle; legend, UNITED STATES OF AMERICA. Exergue, DISME. This was a design for a silver disme.

1792 A copper piece, larger than a dime. Obverse, a bust of Liberty—flowing hair, facing the right; legend, LIBERTY PARENT OF SCIENCE & INDUSTRY; beneath the bust, 1792: reverse, a wreath, within which the words ONE CENT, in two lines across the field; legend, UNITED STATES OF AMERICA. Exergue, $\frac{1}{100}$. A round piece of silver is inserted in the middle of the coin, so that the letter N in the word cent, is stamped upon the silver.

1792 A copper piece, larger than a cent. Obverse, a bust of Washington in military costume;[1] legend, G. WASHINGTON PRESIDENT I, 1792: reverse, a spread eagle, with fifteen stars above its head, in its right talon a bunch of five arrows, and in its left an olive branch; legend, UNITED STATES OF AMERICA. A few specimens of this piece have been found in silver. (See page 59 .)

1792 A silver piece, size of a half dollar. Obverse, a bust of Washington in military costume; legend, G. WASHINGTON PRESIDENT I, 1792: reverse, a spread

[1] A copper piece, with bust of Washington in military costume on each side, " WASHINGTON " over one bust, and " ONE CENT" over the other, is believed to be a modern issue.

eagle, large, in its right talon a bunch of thirteen arrows, in its left an olive branch; legend, UNITED STATES OF AMERICA.

1792   A copper piece, larger than a cent. Obverse, a bust of Washington in military costume; legend, WASHINGTON PRESIDENT, 1792: reverse, a spread eagle, large, holding in its right talon a bundle of thirteen arrows, and in its left an olive branch, a scroll from its beak, inscribed Unum E Pluribus. At the top of the piece a row of thirteen stars.

1792   A copper piece, size of a cent. Obverse, a Roman bust; legend, WASHINGTON PRESIDENT, 1792: reverse, an eagle, spread, holding in its right talon an olive branch, in its left thirteen arrows; the word CENT above its head, and three stars on either side of its neck.

1794   In 1794 and 1795, owing to the scarcity of copper circulation, the mercantile house of Talbot, Allum & Lee, (New York), procured a large quantity of copper coins to be struck in Birmingham, England, which they imported and attempted to put into circulation, but were prevented before they had succeeded to any great extent. These coppers bore the following devices and descriptions: 1. Obverse, a ship in full sail; legend, TALBOT, ALLUM & LEE, ONE CENT; above the ship the words NEW YORK: reverse, a female figure representing liberty, holding in her right hand a staff surmounted by a liberty cap, while her left hand rests on a rudder, a bale of merchandise at her feet; legend, LIBERTY & COM-

MERCE. Exergue, 1794. Edge, PAYABLE AT THE
STORE OF. (Pl. 4, fig. 5.) 2. Obverse, a ship in full
sail; legend, AT THE STORE OF TALBOT, ALLUM &
LEE, NEW YORK: reverse, same as last, except date,
1795. Edge, WE PROMISE TO PAY THE BEARER ONE
CENT.

1796   A silver piece, size of a half dollar. Obverse, a bust
with a laurel wreath, surmounted by a mural crown;
legend, FRANCO–AMERICANA COLONIA; exergue, CAS-
TORLAND, 1796: reverse, a figure of Ceres, holding
in her right hand a cornucopia, and in her left a car-
penter's brace and bit, and at her feet a sheaf of
wheat; she stands near a maple tree, from which
sap is flowing into a tub; a beaver in the exergue;
legend, SALVE MAGNA PARENS FRUGUM. (Pl. 2,
fig. 5.)

This piece is a pattern for a half dollar, struck in
Paris, by Duvivier, for a French settlement in the
northern part of the state of New York, called Cas-
torland.

The following historical facts are intimately connected with it:

On the 31st of August, 1792, William Constable,
one of the three owners of Macomb's great purchase,
sold to Peter Chassanis, of Paris, a large tract of
land in the present counties of Lewis and Jefferson,
east and north of Black river, and intended to contain 640,000 acres, but which upon subsequent survey
was found to fall short several hundred thousand

acres. Chassanis organized a company,[1] which he sent over under the direction of Rodolph Tillier, as agent, about the year 1794. These settlers made the first road north from Steuben to the Black river, and began a settlement in the present town of Greig in Lewis county, adjacent to the High falls. A small beginning was made at the head of navigation on Beaver river, named *Castorville*, and at the present village of Carthage in Jefferson county. The French revolution drove into exile many families of rank and wealth, some of whom settled on this tract, but most of them after a few years returned to France, and the settlements were entirely abandoned.

Further details of this company's operations may be found in Hough's History of Jefferson County.

[1] A pamphlet of the following title was published by Chassanis, in Paris, in 1792, and contains the articles of association of the company organized by him : " Association pour la possession & exploitation de six cens mille acres de terre concédées par l'Etat de New York, & situées dans cet Etat entre les 43e & 44e degrés de latitude sur le Lac Ontario à 35 lieues de la ville & port d'Albany, où abordent les vaisseaux de l'Europe." The pamphlet and some original documents of the company, are in the archives of the New York State Library.

APPENDIX.

CONTENTS.

APPENDIX.

EARLIEST KNOWN COINAGE FOR AMERICA.

The earliest coinage for America is said to have been made in 1612, when the Virginia Company was endeavoring to establish a colony on the Sommer Islands,[1] now better known as the Bermudas. The coin was made of brass with SOMMER ISLAND for a legend, and a Boar for a type, above which XII; reverse, a ship under sail, firing a gun.

COLONIAL LAWS RELATING TO COINAGE.

VIRGINIA.

ACT CONCERNING COINAGE, PASSED 1645.

The Governor, Council and Burgesses of this present Grand Assembly having maturely weighed & considered how advantageous a quoine current would

[1] Snelling gives the following account: "It belongs to the Summer Islands, where a colony was endeavored to be settled under the Virginia Company in 1612, Mr. John More being sent for for that purpose. He was succeeded by Capt. Daniel Necker, in whose time our piece had a currency, as we are informed by Capt. Smith,* who says—'besides meat and drink and cloaths, they had for a time a certaine kind of Brasse money with a Hogge on one side, in memory of the abundance of Hogges which were found on their first landing."

* Hist. Virginia

12

be to this collony, and the great wants and miseries
which do daily happen vnto it by the sole dependency vpon tob'o. have at length resolved and enacted,
and be it by the authoritie aforesaid enacted as the
onely way to procure the said quoine and prevent
the further miseries, That all peeces of eight in
Spanish money be valued and taken in payment, att
the rate of sixe shillings and all other Spanish silver
quoins proportionably which shall be brought into
the collony : And whereas it is conceived that the
said quoine will not continue with vs vnless we have
a leger quoine, Therefore serious consideration had
of the many wayes tending to that effect, It was at
length generally allowed, That a quoine of copper
would be most beneficial to, and with most ease procured by the collony, And that after proclamation
made by the Governour and Council that all person
or persons within this collony whether merchants or
others do desist or leave off tradeing for tob'o. vpon
the penaltie and forfeiture of the thing so bought or
sold, The one moyetie whereof shall be and come to
the informer, and the other to the benefit of the state.

The quoine to be erected after this manner :
10000 lb. of copper to be bought by the publique at
the rate of 18d per lb. which amounts to £750 sterl.
which to be paid in tob'o. at the rate of 1d. 1-2d. per
lb. 120000 of tob'o. which being collected per pole
accounting 5000 in this collony it comes to 24 lb. of
tob'o. per pole every pound of copper to make 20s.
and to allow for the mintage 12d. per pound soe
there will remaine £9500 sterl. The mintage allowed and deducted. The stocke to be equallie divided amongst the adventurers to be quoined in two
pences, three pences, sixe pences and nine pences,
And if it shall happen at any time hereafter that the
aforesaid quoine be called in and become not currant, Yet the republique shall make good the quan-

tity of so much (vizt.) £10000 to be levied per poll, And that it may be provided that this quoine may not be counterfeited and brought in, Besides the inflicting of capitall punishment vpon these who shall be found delinquents therein, That vpon every peece of coyne there be two rings, The one for the motto, The other to receave a new impression which shall be stampted yearly with some new ffigure, by one appointed for that purpose in each county, And that the hon'ble, Sir William Berkeley, Kn't. Gov'r. shall have the disposall and placing of such and soe manie officers as shall necessarilye required for performing and finishing the aforesaid service, Onely Capt. John Upton is hereby confirmed Mint Master Generall : Wee reposing much confidence in his care, abillity and trust for the performance of the said office.

MASSACHUSETTS.

Court Records, 1652—1682.

1652, May 27. It is ordered by this Court & the authoritie thereof, that the printed order about money shalbe in force vntill the first of the seuenth mo[th] next, & no longer ; and that from and after the first of September next, the money hereafter appoynted & expressed shalbe the current money of this common wealth, & no other, vnles English, except the receiuers consent thereunto. In psuance of the intent of this Court herein, be it further ordred and enacted by the authoritie of this Court, that all psons whatsoeuer haue libertie to bring in vnto the mint howse, at Boston, all bullion, plate, or Spanish coyne, there to be melted and brought to the alloy of sterling siluer by John Hull, master of the sd mint, & his sworne officers, & by him to be coyned into twelue pence, six pence, & three pence peeces, which shalbe for forme flatt, & square on the sides, & stamped on the one side with NE, & on the other side with XII^d, VI^d, & III^d, according to the value of each peece, together with a priuie marke, which shalbe appoynted euery three monethes by the Gouernor, & knowne only to him & the sworne officers of the mint ; & further, the sd master of the mint afforesd is hereby required to coyne all the sd money of good siluer of the just alloy of new sterling English money, & for value to stampe two pence in a shilling of lesser valew than the psent English coyne, and the lesser peeces pportionable ; and all such coyne as aforesd shall be acknowledged to be the current coyne of this comon wealth, & pass from man to man in all payment accordingly, within this jurisdiction only. And the mint master, for himselfe & officers, for theire paynes & labour in meltinge, refineinge, & coyninge, is allowed by this Court to take one shillinge out of euery twenty shilling, wch he shall stampe as afforesd. & it shalbe in the liberty of any pson who bring into the mint howse any bullion, plate, or Spanish coyne, as afforesd, to be psent, & se the same melted, refined, & alloyed, & then to take a receit of the master of the mint for the weyght of that which is good siluer, alloyed as aforesd, for which the mint master shall deliuer him the like weight in current money, vizt euery shilling to weigh three penny troy weight and lesser peeces proportionably, deducting allowance for coynage, as before exprest. And that this order beinge of so great concernment, may not in any perticuler thereof fall to the ground, it is further ordered, that Mr. Richard Bellingham, M^r· W^m· Hibbens, the psent secritary, Capt. John Leueritt, & Mr. Thomas Clarke be a comittee appoynted by this Court to appoynt the mint howse in some convenient place in Boston, to giue John Hull, master of the mint, the oath suteable to his place, & to approue of all other officers, & determine what else shall appeare to them as necessary to be done for the carying an end of the whole order, & that all other orders concerning the valuation of coyning of money past this Court shal be repealed.

1652, Oct. 19. For the pvention of washing or cliping all such peeces of money as shalbe coyned within this jurisdiction, it is ordred by this Court & authoritie thereof, that henceforth all peeces of money coyned as afforesd, both shillings and smaller

 peeces, shall haue a double ringe on either side, with this inscription, (Massachusetts), & a tree in the center on the one side, and New England, and the date of the yeare, on the other side, according to this draught heere in the margent.

1652, Oct. 26. The whole Courte, by their generall vote, did allow and approove of the acte of the comittee about minting of money, & respecting their building of the mint howse at the comon charge, and allowance of the officers 15^d in euery twenty shillings for theire paines, and ordered the comittee to continew in theire power till the next eleccon.

1660, October 16. It is ordered, that Capt. Gookin & ye Tresurer, M^r· Anthony Stoddard, & M^r· W^m· Parks shall be a comittee & are hereby impowred to treate wth the mint master for alowing such an annuall some as may be agreed vpon as a meete honorarium to the country for the yearely benefitt they receive by minting, that so the country may reape some bennefitt after so long a forbearance, hauing given them the bennefit thereof for the tjme past, or otherwise to declare that this Court intends to

agree wth some other meete person to minte the
money of this country, making theire report to the
next Court what they shall doe herein.

1661, May 22. Wee haue, according to order,
treated wth the mint masters, Mr. Hull & Mr. Saunderson, & finde them vtterly vnwilling to pay any
certaine proportion to the country of the alllowance
pajd them for coyning money, only they offered tenn
pounds as a free guift to the country, in case they
will please to accept of it; but the comittee refused
that proffer, alleadging that the vse of the mint &
howse required, in justice, some certaine part of the
income receaved by them, w^{ch}, vpon examination,
will be found to be sixty two pounds vpon euery
thousand pounds, out of wch the comittee propounded
they should allow one twentjeth part for the country; but they consented not. This is the present
state of that affaire; leaving it to ye Court to take
such further order therein as vnto them seemes
meete. Dat. 6th June, 1661.

DANIEL GOOKIN,
RICHARD RUSSELL,
ANTHONY STODDARD,
WILLIAM PARKE.

The Court judged it meete to order that this comittee should be reimpowred to treate wth the mint
masters, & to receiue the ten pounds aboue mentioned, & what else they cann get by way of recom-
pence for the mint house for the tjme past, & that
it be deliuered to the Tresurer to be bestowed in
pouder.

1662, May 7. It is ordered by this Court, & the
mint master is hereby enjoyned out of the first bullion that comes to his hand to coyne two penny peeces
of siluer in proportion to the just value & alloy of
other monys allowed heere, to answer the occasions
of the country for exchange: that is, the first yeare
fifty pounds, in such smale money for euery hundred

pounds by him to be coyned, & for aftertime twenty pounds in like smale money annually for euery hundred pounds that shall be coyned: & this order is to continew in force for seuen yeares, any lawe to the contrary notw^th standing.

1667, May 15. Mr. Thomas Danforth, Major Generall Jno. Leueret, Capt. Georg Coruin, Mr. Anthony Stoddard, & M^r· W^m· Parks, are appointed a comittee to treat & agree wth the master or masters of the mint, in refference to some allowance annually, or otherwise, for & in consideration of the charge, the country hath binn at in erecting a mint house, & for the vse of it for so many yeares, wth out any considerable satisfaction, & to make returne thereof to the next session of this Court : and in case they cannot agree wth the present mint masters, they are impowred to make such agreement as they cann wth any other.

1667, Oct. 9.   Boston in New England,
                          October 4th, 1667.

In observance of an order of the Generall Court, held the 15th of May, 1667, nominating & impowring vs, whose names are subscribed, to treat & agree wth the masters of the mint,—wee hauing duely weighed the countrys interest in the ædiffices apperteyning to the sajd office, and agitated the matter wth M^r· Jno. Hull & M^r· Robert Saunderson, the present mint masters, haue agreed wth them as followeth, namely; in consideration of the countrys disbursements on the sajd ædiffices, & for the interest the Generall Court hath therein, to pay vnto the public tresury, wth in six months next coming, forty pounds in money, and for seuen yeares next coming (the sajd Hull & Saunderson, or either of them, personally abiding in the sajd imploy) to allow the public tresury annually in money tenn pounds, the sajd terme to beginne from the date aboue named. In witness hereof the

sajd Hull and Saunderson haue herevnto put their
hands the day & yeare aboue written.

	JNO. LEUERET,
JOHN HULL,	THO. DANFORTH,
ROBERT SANDERSON.	ANTHONY STODDARD,
	WM. PARKE.

The Court thankfully acknowledgeth the good
service of the gent[n] subscribers in the premisses, and
order it to be recorded.

1672, Oct. 8.   Whereas peeces of eight are of more
value to carry out of the country then they will yield
to mint into our coyne, by reason whereof peeces of
eight which might else come to coyning are carrjed
out of the country, it is therefore ordered by this
Court & the authority thereof, that all peeces of
eight that are full weight & good siluer, that is, sixe
shillings of New England money, of Mexico, sevil &
pillar, & so all lesser peeces of each sort, shall passe
in this jurisdiction as current as our oune money
peeces of eight, at sixe shillings a peece, & all lesser
peeces proportionably therevnto, provided that all
such peeces that shall passe in this jurisdiction haue
a stampe affix[t] vpon them, w[ch] shall be NE, to eui-
dence that they are of right allay & due weight; & that
M[r.] John Hull & M[r.] Robert Sanderson, or either of
them be the persons for the tryall & stamping of such
money, & that thereby fower pence vpon the pound
pajd for the rest, one fowerth thereof to the officer,
& the rest, to the country Tresurer.

Whereas peeces of eight, weighing sixe shillings,
are ordered to passe for sixe shillings and ordered
to be stamped, &c, according to the sajd law,
reference thereto being had ; and for as much as
few or no peeces of eight are of that weight, and so
the intent of good to the country therein will be dis-
appointed ; as an addition to the sajd lawe, be it ordered and enacted by this Court & the authority
thereof, that peeces of eight vnder the weight of

sixe shillings shall likewise be passable for so much of New England money as they shall weigh, and that it be impressed vpon the stampe how much each peece doth weigh, in legible figures wth the other letters on ye same, & of the same alloy.

1675, May 12. Whereas the time formerly agreed vpon wth the mint masters is now expired, for the future well setling of that matter, this Court doth desire & impower the honoured Gouner and Magistrates residing in Boston, or any three of them, to be a comittee to treate wth such persons as they shall thinke meet, and to make such an agreement wth them for the coyning of the money of this jurisdiction as may be most incouraging to all persons that haue bullion to bring in the same to the mint.

1675, July 9. In pursuance of an order of the Generall Court, held May the 12th, 1675, relating to the future setting of the mint, it is agreed by vs, the subscribers, as a comittee appointed therevnto, as followeth : i. e.,—

That the former masters of the mint, vizt. Robert Saunderson & John Hull, doe continue to mint what siluer bulljon shall come in for this seven yeares next to come, if either of them liue so long, and doe receive of those that bring bulljon to the mint, as a full reward for their paynes, twelve pence for euery twenty shillings, & three pence for the wast of euery three ounces of sterling siluer that they shall so mint, vizt, fiueteen pence in the whole for every twenty shillings ; and the sajd minters are to pay in to the Treasurer of the country, in mony, twenty pounds p ann during abouesajd terme, That this is our agreement, wittnes our hands heerevnto put, the 3d of June, 1675.

JOHN LEUERET,
LYMAN BRADSTREETE,
EDWARD TYNG,
ROBERT SANDERSON,
JOHN HULL.

13

The Court approooves of this returne, and the set-
lement of the mint accordingly, As attests.

EDWARD RAWSON, Secretary.

1682, May 24.   This Court, taking into consideration that by the frequent exportation of our New
England coyne out of the country, whereby comerce
and trade is very much obstructed, as an expedient
to keepe money in the country, it is ordered, that all
peeces of $\frac{8}{8}$, as pillar, civil, & Mexico coyne, that are
good silver, shall passe amongst us as currant money
of New England, according to their weight in the
present New England coyne.

1682, Oct. 11.   The Court, on the 24th day of May
last, taking into consideration the frequent exportation of our New England cojne out of the countrey,
whereby comerce and trade is very much obstructed,
as an expedient to keepe money in the countrey, did
order, that all peeces of eight as pillar Sevil and
Mexico coyn, that are good siluer, should passe
amongst us as currant money of New England, according to their weight in the present New England
coyn.   As an explanation of that law, it is to be vn-
derstood, and it is heereby declared, that those peeces
of eight in the law mentioned shallbe pajd and received at sixe shillings eight pence p ounce troy
weight, and all smaller peeces of the like coyn that
are good siluer shall passe at the same price & weight.

1697, Oct.   *An Act for ascertaining the value of coins
current within this province.*   Whereas for many years
past the money coined in the late Massachusetts
colony hath passed current at the rate or value it
was stamped for, and good Sevil, pillar, or Mexico
pieces of eight of full seventeen pennyweight, have
also passed current at six shillings per piece, and
half pieces of proportionable weight pro rata, quarter pieces of the same coin at sixteen pence per piece,
and reals of the same coin at eight pence per piece,

Be it therefore enacted and declared by the lieutenant governor, council and representatives convened in general assembly, and by the authority of the same, that all and every the coins before mentioned shall still be and continue current money within this province, and shall be accepted, taken and received, at the respective values aforesaid, according as hath heretofore been accustomed,

Provided alway, that such of the said coins as pass by tale be not diminished by washing, clipping, rounding, filing or scaling.

MARYLAND.

The Freemen (1) set forth in the Preamble, that the want of money is a great Hindrance to the Advancement of this Colony, in Trade, &c., humbly praying his Lordship to take order for the setting up of a Mint, for the Coining of Money, within this Province. (2.) It was enacted, That the money coined therein should be of as good Silver as English sterling money. (3.) Every shilling so coined, to weigh above Nine Pence, in such Silver, and other Pieces in Proportion. (4.) Every offence of clipping scaling, counterfeiting, washing, or any way diminishing such coin to be punished with Death, and Forfeiture of Lands, Goods, &c., to the said Lord Propritary. (5.) His Lordship to take and accept the said Coin in Payment for his Rents, Arrears of Rent and all other Engagements due to his Lordship, &c., according to this Act.

AN ACT FOR THE ADVANCEMENT OF COIN, PASSED NOV. 19, 1686.

Sets forth in the Preamble the great want of ready money, whereby the trade of the Province and settlement of Handicrafts and Tradesmen therein was much impeded, & Enacts (1.) That New England shillings & sixpences shall pass as sterling, (viz. at the advance of 3d in each shilling) French Crowns, Piece of Eight, and Rix Dollars to pass at 6s., Ducatoons at 7s. 6d, and all other coins of silver or gold, foreign or not foreign, except base coin, to be taken and received with the advance of 3d sterling, in the value of 12d. sterling.

LAWS RELATING TO COINAGE, DURING THE PERIOD OF THE CONFEDERATION.

CONNECTICUT.

AT A GENERAL ASSEMBLY OF THE STATE OF CONNECTICUT, HOLDEN AT NEW HAVEN IN SAID STATE, ON THE SECOND THURSDAY OF OCTOBER, ANNO DOM. 1785.

Upon the Memorial of Samuel Bishop, Joseph Hopkins, James Hillhouse, and John Goodrich praying for Liberty to establish a Mint for Coining Copper in this State under the direction and superintendance of the General Assembly, they paying one twentieth part of all Copper by them Coined into the Treasury of this State to and for the Use of this State as p^r Memorial on file &c, Resolved by this Assembly that said Samuel Bishop, Joseph Hopkins, James Hillhouse & John Goodrich have Liberty, and Liberty and Authority is hereby granted to them to establish a Mint for Coining and Manufacturing Coppers not to exceed the amount of ten thousand pounds lawfull Money in value of the Standard of British half pence to weigh six penny weight and to bear

the following Impression or Stamp viz a Mans Head
on the One side with a Circumscription in the Words
or Letters following viz Auctori : Connec :, and on
the other side the Emblem of Liberty with an Olive
Branch in her Hand with a Circumscription in the
Words and Figures following viz Inde: Et: Lib: 1785:
which Grant is to continue during the pleasure of
the General Assembly not exceeding five Years, the
Memorialists paying into the Treasury of this State
at the end of every six months one twentieth part of
all Coppers by them Coined or Manufactured at said
Mint, The Memorialists are not however to put off
or into Circulation any Coppers by them Coined un-
till the same shall have been Inspected and approved
by the Honble Roger Sherman and James Wadsworth Esq^rs, David Austin Esqr and Messrs Ebenezer
Chittenden & Isaac Beers or the Major part of them
who are hereby appointed a Committee for that purpose or such other Committee as the General Assembly shall from Time to Time appoint, such Inspection
to be made at the expence of the Memorialists, Provided nothing in this Act shall be construed to make
such Coppers a legal Tender in payment of any
Debts.

VERMONT.

AN ACT GRANTING TO REUBEN HARMON JUNIOR, ESQ., A RIGHT OF COINING COPPER, AND REGULATING THE SAME, PASSED JUNE 15, 1785.

Whereas Reuben Harmon Junior Esqr. of Ruport
in the County of Bennington, by his Petition has
represented that he has purchased a quantity of
Copper, suitable for Coining, and praying this Legislature to grant him a right to coin Copper, under

such regulations as this Assembly shall think meet ;
and this Assembly being willing to incourage an undertaking that promises so much public utility, therefore :

Be it enacted, and it is hereby enacted by the Representatives of the Freemen of the State of Vermont
in General Assembly met and by the authority of the
same ; that there be and hereby is granted to the
said Reuben Harmon Junior Esqr, the exclusive right
of coining Copper within this State ; for the term of
two years from the first day of July in the present
year of our Lord one thousand seven hundred and
eighty-five : and all Coppers by him coined, shall be
in pieces of one third of an ounce, Troy weight each,
with such Devices and Mottos as shall be agreed
upon by the Committee appointed for that purpose
by this Assembly.

And be it further enacted by the authority aforesaid that the said Reuben Harmon before he enter on
the business of coining, or take any benefit of this
act, shall enter into a bond of five thousand pounds,
to the Treasurer of this State ; with two or more
good and sufficient sureties, Freeholders of this State,
conditioned that all the Copper, by him coined as
aforesaid, shall be of full weight as specified in this
act, and that the same shall be made of good and
genuine Metal.

AN ACT GRANTING TO REUBEN HARMON, JUN. ESQ. THE RIGHT OF COIN-
ING COPPER WITHIN THIS STATE, FOR A FARTHER TERM OF EIGHT
YEARS, PASSED 1786.

Whereas, the Legislature of this State did, at
their sessions at Norwich, in June, 1785, grant to
Reuben Harmon, jun, Esq. of Ruport, in the county
of Bennington, the exclusive right of coining copper
within this State, for the term of two years from the
first day of July, in the aforesaid year of our Lord,

1785; and whereas, the said Reuben has, by his petition, represented to this Assembly, that he has been at great expense in erecting works and procuring a quantity of copper for the purpose of carrying on said business of coining and that by reason of the shortness of said term, he will be unable to indemnify himself for his said expense; and praying this Assembly to grant him said privilege of coining copper for a longer term; and this Assembly willing to encourage an undertaking that promises a considerable public utility, Therefore, *Be it enacted, &c.* that there be, and hereby is granted and confirmed to the said Reuben Harmon, jun. Esq. the exclusive right of coining copper within this State, for a farther term of eight years from the first day of July, in the year of our Lord, 1787; and that all copper by him coined, shall be in pieces weighing not less than four penny weight fifteen grains each; and the device for all copper, by him hereafter coined, shall be, on the one side, a head with the motto, *auctoritate Vermontensium* abridged—on the reverse, a woman, with the letters, INDE: ET LIB: for Independence and Liberty.

And be it fu ther enacted, that the said Reuben shall have and enjoy the aforesaid privilege of coining copper within this State, free from any duty to this State as a compensation thereof, for the full term of three years from the first day of July, in the year of our Lord, 1787; and that, from and after the expiration of the said three years, he the said Reuben shall pay for the use of the State, two and one half per cent, of all the copper he shall coin for and during the remainder of the aforesaid term of eight years: and the said Reuben, before he take any benefit of this act, shall enter into a bond of five thousand pounds, to the treasurer of this State, with two or more good and sufficient sureties, freeholders of this State, conditioned that all the copper, by him coined as aforesaid, shall be of full weight as specified in this act, and of genuine metal, and that from and after the expiration of the aforesaid three years, he will well and truly render an account of the sums by him coined, by virtue of this grant, and pay over all such sums as shall, on account of said coinage, become due to this State, at such times, and in such manner, as this or a future Assembly shall direct.

NEW JERSEY.

AN ACT FOR THE ESTABLISHMENT OF A COINAGE OF COPPER IN THIS STATE, PASSED JUNE 1, 1786.

Whereas the Copper Coin now Current and passing in this State consists mostly of base metal, and of coppers so small and light as to be of very little real value, Whereby the citizens of this State are subjected to manifest loss and inconvenience and are liable to be greatly defrauded ; for remedy whereof,

Sect. 1.   Be it enacted by the Council and General Assembly of this State, and it is hereby Enacted by the authority of the same, That Walter Mould Thomas Goadsby and Albion Cox, and the Survivors and Survivor of them are hereby authorized and Empowered, from and after the publication of this Act, to strike and coin in copper, for this State, a sum Equal in value to Ten Thousand Pounds at fifteen Coppers to the Shilling.

2. And be it further Enacted by the authority aforesaid, that the Coppers so to be coined shall be of pure Copper, and of the Weight of six pennyweight and six grains ; that they shall be manufactured and coined within this State, and shall have such Marks and Inscriptions as shall be directed by the Justices of the Supreme Court, or any one of them.

3. And be it further Enacted by the Authority aforesaid, that the said Coppers, so to be struck and coined shall be of the value aforesaid, unless the United States in Congress assembled shall by a publick Act, alter the valuation thereof, to which alteration the value thereof shall at all times be subject.

4. And be it further Enacted by the authority aforesaid, That the said Walter Mould, Thomas Goadsby and Albion Cox, before they shall enter on or begin the Coinage aforesaid, shall enter into bond to the Governor or Commander in Chief of this State, to the use of the State, with at least two sufficient sureties, in the sum of Ten Thousand Pounds, conditioned that the said Walter Mould, Thomas Goadsby and Albion Cox, or one or more of them, shall, within two Years after the Publication of this Act, strike and coin, within this State, the full sum of ten thousand Pounds in Coppers as aforesaid, and that they shall faithfully and honestly demean themselves in Coining said Coppers ; and that they will deliver to the Treasurer of this State, or his order, for the use of the State, one tenth part of the full sum they shall strike and coin as aforesaid, which said tenth part shall be paid quarterly unto the Treasurer as aforesaid, by the said Walter Mould, Thomas Goadsby and Albion Cox, from the time they shall begin to coin as aforesaid during the time they may carry on said business ; which Bond the Treasurer is authorized and Empowered to take and the same to file in the Auditor's Office : And the said Walter Mould, Thomas Goadsby and Albion Cox, shall, at the Time of giving said Bond, respectively take an Oath or Affirmation that they will well and truly account to the Legislature for the tenth part of all the Coppers they may coin as aforesaid, and that they will truly and faithfully Execute the said coinage agreeably to the true Intent and Meaning of this Act.

14

5. And be it further Enacted, That if any Person or Persons whatsoever shall strike or coin any Coppers within this State, without leave being first had and obtained from the Legislature to do the same, he shall forfeit and pay for each day he or they may be so Employed in striking or coining Coppers contrary to the true Intent and Meaning of the Act, the sum of Twelve Pounds, to be recovered by the Collector of the County in an Action of debt in any Court within which the same may be Cognizable, with Costs of Suit, to be paid into the Treasury of the State for the Time being for the use of the State.

A SUPPLEMENTARY ACT TO THE ACT INTITLED AN ACT FOR THE ES-
TABLISHMENT OF A COINAGE OF COPPER IN THIS STATE, PASSED
NOV. 22, 1786.

Whereas by an Act Passed at Brunswick the first day of June last, intitled An Act for the Establishment of a coinage of Copper in this State, Walter Mould, Thomas Goadsby and Albion Cox, were jointly nominated to Execute the said business, subject to certain Conditions, Restrictions and Penalties : And whereas it appears that delays have been occasioned, and the good intentions of the before mentioned Act is likely to be defeated by the circumstances of the Parties being jointly bound to Execute the Contract, therefore, in order to facilitate and forward the Business agreeably to, and on the Terms prescribed by said Act,

Sect. 1. Be it Enacted by the Council and General Assembly of the State and it is hereby Enacted by the authority of the same, That it shall and may be lawful for the said Thomas Goadsby and Albion Cox, from and after the Publication of this Act, to proceed in the Coinage of two third parts of the sum authorized in the Act intitled An Act for the Establishment of a Coinage of Copper in this State, to wit, of six thousand six hundred and sixty six Pounds, thirteen shillings and four-Pence in as full and ample a manner as they might have done under the former Act, had the said Walter Mould joined himself to and subscribed the Conditions and Penalties enjoined by said Act.

Provided nevertheless, and it is hereby understood and required, That, previous to the Entering upon the Business aforesaid, they the said Thomas Goadsby and Albion Cox, give and enter into like Bonds, and take the same Oath as is prescribed by the before mentioned Act, Excepting only so far as relates to the joining of the said Walter Mould to the said Thomas Goadsby and Albion Cox, and also that they be subject to the like Limitations and Restrictions with those pointed out in the said Act.

3. And be it further Enacted by the Authority aforesaid, That the said Walter Mould be, and he is hereby authorized and Empowered to begin and enter upon the Coinage of the remaining Three Thousand Three Hundred and Thirty three Pounds six shillings and Eight-Pence, upon his previously taking the like Oath, and giving a seperate Bond in his own name, with two Sufficient Sureties for the same sum, and under the same Restrictions, Conditions and Penalties with those required from the said Walter Mould, Thomas Goadsby and Albion Cox in the before recited Act. Provided Always, That in Case of Neglect, Refusal or Failure on the part of the said Walter Mould, to comply with the above Conditions, and enter upon the coinage of the above mentioned one third—within two months from the date hereof, it shall and may in that case be lawful for the said Thomas Goadsby and Albion Cox to take upon themselves solely the whole Coinage of the sum of Ten Thousand Pounds, as fully and Amply and under the same Exclusive Conditions and Restrictions, as Wal-

ter Mould, Thomas Goadsby and Albion Cox, were by the former Act Empowered jointly to do.

4. And be it further Enacted by the Authority aforesaid, That if they, or either of them, neglect to give bond as aforesaid, he or they so neglecting shall be made liable to forfeit and pay the same sum, to be recovered in the same manner that other Persons are made liable to pay for striking or Coining Coppers, by the before recited Act.

AN ACT TO PREVENT THE CIRCULATION OF BAD AND LIGHT COPPERS IN THIS STATE, PASSED JUNE 4, 1787.

WHEREAS, the Circulation of Coppers which are of base Metal, and below the proper Standard, must be productive of great Evils to the commercial Part of this State, if not timely prevented ; therefore,

BE IT ENACTED by the Council and General Assembly of this State, and it is hereby Enacted by the authority of the same, That if any Person or Persons, from and after the twentieth Day of July next, shall pass or offer to pass in Payment, or in Exchange within this State, any Coppers other than those made within the same, agreeable to Permission given by a Law passed the first Day of June, One Thousand Seven Hundred and Eighty-six, and the Supplement thereto, passed the twenty-second Day of November, in the same Year, each and every Person or Persons, so offending, shall forfeit and pay ten Times the nominal Value of the Sum or Sums so offered in Payment, or in Exchange, to be recovered by Action of Debt, by any Person that will sue for and recover the same, with Cost of Suit, to and for his own Use: *Provided*, That Nothing in this Act contained shall be construed to extend to any Copper Coin that shall be struck by the United States of America in Congress assembled.

MASSACHUSETTS.

AN ACT FOR ESTABLISHING A MINT FOR THE COINAGE OF GOLD, SILVER
AND COPPER, PASSED OCT. 17, 1786.

Whereas the United States in Congress assembled, by their resolve of the eighth day of August, in the present year, have regulated the alloy and value of coin; and whereas the want of a sufficient circulating medium renders it expedient, that a mint should be erected and a quantity of coin be struck; therefore,

Be it enacted by the Senate and House of Representatives, in General Court assembled, and by the authority of the same, That there shall be a mint erected within this Commonwealth, for the coinage of gold, silver and copper; and that all the coin, that shall be struck therein, shall be of the same weight, alloy and value, and each piece bear the same name, as is by the said resolve of Congress fixed and established.

And be it further enacted by the authority aforesaid, That there shall be a quantity of copper coin struck, equal to the amount of *seventy thousand dollars*, in pieces of the two different denominations mentioned in the said resolve, and in convenient proportions; one of which to have the name *cent* stamped in the centre thereof, and the other *half* cent, with such inscription or devices as the Government with the advice of Council, may think proper, and the said coin when struck, shall be received in all payments in this Commonwealth.

And be it further enacted, That the Governor with the advice of Council be, and he is hereby authorized and empowered to appoint some suitable person or persons, to procure all the necessaries requisite to the completing of the said mint, fit for coining, and to take due care that the same be completed as soon as may be, and also to procure an able assay master, stock, workmen, and whatever may be necessary for the actual coinage of gold, silver and copper, as before directed ; and the Governor with the advice of Council, is hereby further empowered to appoint some suitable person or persons to have the oversight and inspection of the said mint when completed, and to see to the coinage of the copper afore mentioned, and of the gold and silver that may be bought in for stock or brought in for coining. And the Governor with the advice of Council, is hereby further empowered to establish rules and regulations, respecting the well ordering and managing the business of the said mint, for the safe keeping the stock and coin that may be kept therein, and for. securing the fidelity of all employed in the said business. And the inspector or inspectors appointed as aforesaid, shall before he or they enter on the business of said appointment, give bonds for the faithful discharge of the duties of the appointment, with sureties to the Treasurer of the Commonwealth, in such coin or sums, as the Governor with the advice of Council shall direct.

And be it further enacted, That all the gold, silver and copper belonging to the Commonwealth, that may from time to time be coined in the said mint, so often as the same shall amount to the value of *one thousand dollars*, shall be delivered by the said inspector or inspectors into the treasury of this Commonwealth, he or they taking duplicate receipts therefor, one of which shall be lodged in the Secretary's office.

And be it further enacted, That the charge of erecting and completing the said mint, of stock, workmen, officers, and all other disbursements for carrying on the said business of coining, shall be defrayed out of the said coin, by warrant of the Governor, with advice of Council; the accounts relating to the said mint and the business thereof, having been first attested by the inspector or inspectors, and laid before the Council, examined and approved. And if there should remain any sum or sums of money arising from the said coinage, more than is necessary for the payment of the aforesaid expenditures, the same shall be appropriated to the purchase of stock for the said mint, unless the General Court shall otherwise order.

And be it further enacted, That the inspector or inspectors of the said mint, shall from time to time lay before the Governor and Council an account of their doings, and state of the said mint, that the same may be laid before the General Court.

UNITED STATES CONGRESS.

From the Journals of Congress.

1782, Feb. 21. On the Report of a committee of the States consisting of Mr. Livermore, Mr. Patridge, Mr. Cornell, Mr. Wolcott, Mr. Floyd, Mr. Clark, Mr. Clymer, Mr. Carroll, Mr. J. Jones, Mr. Hawkins, Mr. Middleton, Mr. Telfair, to whom was referred a letter of the 15th of January, from the superintendent of finance, touching the establishment of the mint :

Resolved, That Congress approve of the establishment of a mint ; and, that the superintendent of Finance be, and hereby is directed to prepare and report to Congress a plan for establishing and conducting the same.

1785, July 6. Resolved, That the money unit of the United States of America be one dollar.

Resolved, That the smallest coin be a copper, of which 200 shall pass for one dollar.

Resolved, That the several pieces shall increase in a decimal ratio.

1786, Aug. 8.   Resolved, That the standard of the United States of America, for gold and silver, shall be eleven parts fine and one part alloy.

That the money unit of the United States, being by a resolve of Congress of the 6th July, 1785, a dollar shall contain of fine silver, $375 \frac{64}{100}$ grains.

That the money of account, to correspond with the division of coins, agreeably to the above resolve, proceed in a decimal ratio, agreeably to the forms and manner following, viz.

Mills: The lowest money of account, of which
    1000 shall be equal to the federal dollar, or
    money unit,............................. 0.001
Cents : The highest copper piece, of which 100
    shall be equal to the dollar,.............., 0.010
Dimes : The lowest silver coin, 10 of which shall
    be equal to the dollar,.................. 0.100
Dollar : The highest silver coin,............, 1.000

That betwixt the dollar and the lowest copper coin as fixed by the resolve of Congress of the 6th July, 1785, there shall be three silver coins, and one copper coin.

That the silver coins shall be as follows : one coin containing $187 \frac{82}{100}$ grains of fine silver, to be called A Half Dollar : one coin containing $75 \frac{128}{1000}$ grains of fine silver, to be called A Double Dime : And one coin containing $37 \frac{560}{1000}$ grains of fine silver, to be called A Dime.

That the two copper coins shall be as follows: one equal to the 100th part of the federal dollar, to be called A Cent : And one equal to the 200th part of the federal dollar to be called A Half Cent,

That two pounds and a quarter avoirdupois weight of copper, shall constitute 100 cents.

That there shall be two gold coins: One containing 246 $\frac{268}{1000}$ grains of fine gold, equal to 10 dollars, to be stamped with the impression of the American Eagle, and to be called An Eagle: one containing 123 $\frac{134}{1000}$ grains of fine gold, equal to 5 dollars, to be stamped in like manner, and to be called A Half Eagle.

That the mint price of a pound troy weight of uncoined silver, 11 parts fine and one part alloy shall be 9 dollars, 9 dimes and 2 cents.

That the mint price of a pound troy weight of uncoined gold, 11 parts fine and one part alloy, shall be 209 dollars, 7 dimes and 7 cents.

Ordered, That the Board of Treasury report a draft of an ordinance for the establishment of a mint.

AN ORDINANCE FOR THE ESTABLISHMENT OF A MINT OF THE UNITED STATES OF AMERICA, AND FOR REGULATING THE VALUE AND ALLOY OF OF COIN.

1786, Oct. 16. It is hereby ordained by the United States in Congress assembled, that a mint be established for the coinage of gold, silver and copper money, agreeably to the resolves of Congress of the 8th August last, under the direction of the following officers, viz :

An Assay Master, whose duty it shall be to receive gold and silver in bullion, or foreign coin, to assay the same and to give his certificates for the value thereof at the following rates:

For every pound troy weight of uncoined gold or foreign gold coin, 11 parts fine and one part alloy, 209 dollars, 7 dimes and 7 cents, money of the United States, as established by the resolves of Congress of the 8th of August last, and so in proportion to the

15

fine gold contained in any coined or uncoined gold whatsoever.

For every pound troy weight of uncoined silver, or foreign silver coin, 11 parts fine and one part alloy, 13 dollars, 7 dimes, 7 cents and 7 mills, money of the United States, established as aforesaid : and so in proportion to the fine silver contained in any coined or uncoined silver whatsoever.

A Master Coiner, whose duty it shall be to receive from time to time, of the assay master, the bullion necessary for coinage ; to report to Congress devices and proofs of the proposed pieces of coin, and to procure proper workmen to execute the business of coinage, reporting from time to time, to the commissioners of the board of treasury of the United States for approbation and allowance, the occupation, number and pay of the persons so employed.

A Pay Master, who shall be the treasurer of the United States for the time being, whose duty it shall be to receive and take charge of the coin made under the direction of the master coiner, and to receipt for the same : to receive and duly enter the certificates for uncoined gold or silver issued by the assay-master, and to pay $\frac{95}{100}$ of the amount thereof in gold or silver, and $\frac{5}{100}$ in the copper coin of the United States.

And it is hereby further ordained, That the certificates to be given by the assay master, to persons who shall lodge gold or silver in the mint for coinage, shall be on fine blank paper, and expressed in the manner and form following, to wit :

Mint of the United States.

I acknowledge to have received of A. B. for coinage, (here insert the weight) of (insert the species) bullion, for the amount of which pay to   or

bearer, the sum of   at ten days sight, agreeably
to the custom of the mint.

C. D., Assay Master.
To E. F., Pay-Master of the Mint of the United States of America.

It is hereby further ordained, That the officers above
mentioned, shall settle their accounts monthly, agreeably to such forms and vouchers as shall be prescribed by the comptroller of the Treasury.

And it is hereby further ordained, That the officers
shall enter into bonds to the United States in Congress assembled, for the faithful execution of the
trust respectively reposed in them, in the manner
and amount following, viz :

The Assay-Master, in the sum of 10,000 dollars,
and two sureties, each in the sum of 5000 dollars.

The Master Coiner, in the sum of 10,000 dollars,
and two sureties, each in the sum of 5000 dollars.

And that the officers mentioned in this ordinance
as well as every other person employed in the mint,
shall take and subscribe the oath of office, established by the resolve of the 14th March, 1786.*

And it is hereby further ordained, That it shall be
the duty of the comptroller of the treasury to report
monthly to the commissioners of the treasury of the
United States, a statement of the mint accounts adjusted agreeably to the usual forms ; and if on such
statement or other information it shall appear, that
there has been any neglect, mismanagement or abuse
of trust, in any of the officers mentioned in the within
ordinance, it shall be the duty of the commissioners
of the board of treasury to suspend such officer or
officers, and to report thereon specially to Congress.

---

* Resolved, That in all cases where an oath of office is required of
any person holding an office under the United States in Congress assembled, such oath be in the form of the oath of office established in
the ordinance for ascertaining the powers and duties of the Secretary
at war, passed the 27th day of Jan. 1785. *Mutatis mutandis.*

It is hereby further ordained, That the copper struck under the authority of the United States in Congress assembled, shall be receivable in all taxes, or payments due to the United States, in the proportion of 5 dollars for every hundred dollars so paid ; but that no other copper coin whatsoever, shall be receivable in any taxes or payments whatsoever to the United States.

And whereas, The great quantities of base copper daily imported into, or manufactured within the several states, is become so highly injurious to the interest and commerce of the same, as to require the immediate interposition of the powers vested by the confederation in the United States in Congress assembled, of regulating the value of copper, the coin so current as aforesaid.

It is hereby ordained, That no foreign copper coin whatsoever, shall, after the first day of September, 1787, be current within the U. States of America : And that no copper coin struck under the authority of a particular state, shall pass at a greater value than one federal dollar for two pounds and one quarter of a pounds, avoirdupois weight, of such copper coin.

1786, Oct. 17. Resolved, That the assay-master, to be appointed under the ordinance passed yesterday for the establishment of a mint for the United States, shall be allowed 600 dollars, and the master coiner 1000 dollars per annum.

1787, July 6. Resolved, That the Board of Treasury direct the Contractor for the copper coinage to stamp on one side of each piece the following device, viz : Thirteen circles linked together, a small circle in the middle, with the motto "United States" round it : and in the centre, the words "We are one" : on the other side of the same piece the following devices, viz : A dial with the hours expressed on the face of it : a meridian seen above, on one side of which is to be the word "fugio," and on the other the year in figures "1787."

1791, March 3. Resolved by the Senate and House of Representatives of the United States of America in Congress assembled, That a mint shall be established under such regulations as shall be directed by law.

Resolved, That the President of the United States be, and he is hereby authorized to cause to be engaged, such principal artists as shall be necessary to carry the preceding resolution into effect, and to stipulate the terms and conditions of their service, and also to cause to be procured such apparatus as shall be requisite for the same purpose.

UNITED STATES.

LAWS RELATING TO THE MINT.

I. OFFICERS OF THE MINT,

1. That a mint for the purpose of a national coinage be and the same is established; to be situate and carried on at the seat of government of the United States, for the time being.—*Act April* 2, 1792.

2. That the act, entitled "An act concerning the mint," approved March the 3d, 1801,[1] be and the same hereby is revived and continued in force and operation, until otherwise provided by law.—*Act May* 19, 1828.

3. The officers of the mint of the United States shall be a director, a treasurer, an assayer, a melter and refiner, a chief coiner and an engraver, to be appointed by the president of the United States, by

[1] This act directed that the mint should remain in Philadelphia until March 4, 1803.

and with the advice and consent of the senate.—*Act Jan.* 18, 1837.

4. The respective duties of the officers of the mint shall be as follows:

First. The director shall have the control and management of the mint, the superintendence of the officers and persons employed therein and the general regulation and supervision of the business of the several branches. And in the month of January of every year he shall make report to the president of the United States of the operations of the mint and its branches for the year preceding; and also to the secretary of the treasury, from time to time, as said secretary shall require, setting forth all the operations of the mint subsequent to the last report made upon the subject.

5. Second. The treasurer shall receive and safely keep all moneys which shall be for the use and support of the mint; shall keep all the current accounts of the mint, and pay all moneys due by the mint, on warrants from the director; he shall receive all bullion brought to the mint for coinage; shall be the keeper of all bullion and coin in the mint, except while the same is legally placed in the hands of other officers; and shall, on warrants from the director, deliver all coins struck at the mint to the person or persons to whom they shall be legally payable. And he shall keep regular and faithful accounts of all the transactions of the mint, in bullion and coins, both with the officers of the mint and the depositors; and shall present, quarter-yearly, to the treasury department of the United States, according to such forms as shall be prescribed by that department, an account of the receipts and disbursements of the mint, for the purpose of being adjusted and settled.

6. Third. The assayer shall carefully assay all metals used in coinage, whenever such assays are required in the operations of the mint; and he shall

also make assays of coins whenever instructed to do so by the director.

7. Fourth. The melter and refiner shall execute all the operations which are necessary in order to form ingots of standard silver or gold, suitable for the chief coiner, from the metals legally delivered to him for that purpose.

8. Fifth. The chief coiner shall execute all the operations which are necessary in order to form coins, conformably in all respects to the law, from the standard silver and gold ingots [and the copper planchets,] legally delivered to him for this purpose.

9. Sixth. The engraver shall prepare and engrave, with the legal devices and inscriptions, all the dies used in the coinage of the mint and its branches.

10. The director shall appoint, with the approbation of the president, assistants to the assayer, melter and refiner, chief coiner and engraver, and clerks for the director and treasurer, whenever, on representation made by the director to the president, it shall be the opinion of the president that such assistants or clerks are necessary. And it shall be the duty of the assistants to aid their principals in the execution of their respective offices, and of the clerks to perform such duties as shall be prescribed for them by the director.

11. Whenever any officer of the mint shall be temporarily absent, on account of sickness, or any other sufficient cause, it shall be lawful for the director, with the assent of said officer, to appoint some person attached to the mint, to act in the place of such officer during his absence; and the director shall employ such workmen and servants in the mint as he shall from time [to time] find necessary.

12. Every officer, assistant and clerk of the mint, shall, before he enters upon the execution of his office, take an oath or affirmation before some judge of the United States, or judge of the superior court

or any court of record of any state, faithfully and diligently to perform the duties thereof.

13. The following officers of the mint, before entering upon the execution of their respective offices, shall become bound to the United States, with one or more sureties, to the satisfaction of the secretary of the treasury, in the sums hereinafter mentioned, with the condition for the faithful and diligent performance of the duties of their offices, viz : the treasurer in the sum of ten thousand dollars; the assayer in the sum of five thousand dollars; the melter and refiner in the sum of ten thousand dollars ; the chief coiner in the sum of ten thousand dollars. And similar bonds may also be required of the assistants and clerks, in such sums as the director shall determine, with the approbation of the secretary of the treasury.

14. There shall be allowed to the officers of the mint the following salaries per annum : to the director for his services, including traveling expenses incurred in visiting the different branches, and all other charges whatever, three thousand five hundred dollars ; to the treasurer, assayer, melter and refiner, chief coiner and engraver, each two thousand dollars; to the assistants and clerks, such annual salaries shall be allowed as the director may determine, with the approbation of the president : *Provided*, That an assistant shall not receive more than fifteen hundred dollars ; and that a clerk shall not receive more than twelve hundred dollars. To the workmen and servants shall be allowed such wages, to be determined by the director, as may be customary and reasonable according to their respective stations and occupations ; and the salaries provided for in this section shall be payable in quarterly instalments.

15. That the seventh section of the act of January 18th, 1837, entitled "An act supplementary to the

act entitled 'An act establishing a mint and regulating the coins of the United States,'" be so amended as to extend the limit of the annual salary of clerks in the mint of the Uuited States to eighteen hundred dollars each, from and after the first of July, 1854, at the discretion of the officers authorized by law to appoint, with the approbation of the president of the United States, including also one clerk in the office of the assistant treasurer at Philadelphia; and the salary of the chief clerk of the branch mint at New Orleans, shall be twenty-two hundred dollars from and after the first of July, 1854.—*Act August 4, 1854.*

16. The director of the mint shall make his annual report to the secretary of the treasury, up to the thirtieth of June in each year, so that the same may appear in his annual report to congress on the finances.—*Act Feb.* 21, 1857.

II. ASSAY AND COINAGE OF BULLION.

17. It shall be lawful for the director of the mint to receive, and cause to be assayed, bullion not intended for coinage, and to cause certificates to be given of the fineness thereof by such officer as he shall designate for that purpose, at such rates of charge to be paid by the owner of said bullion, and under such regulations as the said director may from time to time establish.—*Act May* 19, 1828.

18. Gold and silver bullion brought to the mint for coinage, shall be received and coined by the proper officers, for the benefit of the depositor: *Provided*, That it shall be lawful to refuse at the mint, any deposit of less value than one hundred dollars, and any bullion so base as to be unsuitable for the operations of the mint: *And provided also*, That when gold and silver are combined, if either of these metals be in such small proportion that it can not be sepa-

16

rated advantageously, no allowance shall be made to the depositor for the value of such metal.—*Act Jan.* 18, 1837.

19. When bullion is brought to the mint for coinage, it shall be weighed by the treasurer in the presence of the depositor, when parcticable, and a receipt given, which shall state the description and weight of the bullion : *Provided,* That when bullion is in such a state as to require melting before its value can be ascertained, the weight after melting shall be considered as the true weight of the bullion deposited.

20. From every parcel of bullion deposited for coinage, the treasurer shall deliver to the assayer a sufficient portion for the purpose of being assayed ; but all such bullion remaining from the operations of the assay shall be returned to the treasurer by the assayer.

21. The assayer shall report to the treasurer the quality or standard of the bullion assayed by him ; and he shall also communicate to the treasurer such information as will enable him to estimate the amount of the charges hereinafter provided for, to be made to the depositor, for the expenses of converting the bullion into standard metal fit for coinage.

22. The only subjects of charge by the mint to the depositor shall be the following :[1] for refining when the bullion is below standard ; for toughening when metals are contained in it which render it unfit for coinage ; for copper used for alloy when the bullion is above standard; for silver introduced into the alloy of gold ; and for separating the gold and silver when these metals exist together in the bullion.   And the rate of these charges shall be fixed from time to time by the director, with the concurrence of the secretary of the treasury, so as not to exceed, in their judgment, the actual expense to the

See *infra,* 42, 43.

mint of the materials and labor employed in each of the cases aforementioned ; and the amount received from these charges shall be accounted for and appropriated for defraying the contingent expenses of the mint.

23. From the report of the assayer, and the weight of the bullion, the treasurer shall estimate the whole value of each deposit, and also the amount of the charges or deductions if any ; of all which he shall give a detailed memorandum to the depositor ; and he shall also give, at the same time, under his hand, a certificate of the net amount of the deposit, to be paid in coins of the same species of bullion as that deposited.

24. Parcels of bullion shall be from time to time transferred by the treasurer to the melter and refiner ; a careful record of these transfers, noting the weight and character of the bullion, shall be kept ; and the bullion thus placed in the hands of the melter and refiner shall be subjected to the several processes which may be necessary to form it into ingots of the legal standard, and of a quality suitable for coinage.

25. The ingots thus prepared shall be assayed by the assayer, and if they prove to be within the limits allowed for deviation from the standard, they shall be transferred by the melter and refiner to the treasurer, accompanied by the assayer's certificate of their fineness ; and a careful record of the transfer shall be kept by the treasurer.

26. No ingots of gold shall be used for coinage of which the quality differs more than two-thousandths from the legal standard ; and no ingots of silver shall be used for coinage of which the quality differs more than three-thousandths from the legal standard.

27. In the treasurer's account with the melter

and refiner, the melter and refiner shall be debited with the standard weight of all the bullion placed in his hands, that is to say, with the weight of metal of legal standard fineness which it will make ; and he shall be credited by the standard weight of all the ingots delivered by him to the treasurer. And once at least in every year, at such time as the director shall appoint, the melter and refiner shall deliver up to the treasurer all the bullion in his possession, in order that his accounts may be settled up to that time ; and, in this settlement, he shall be entitled to a credit for the difference between the whole amount of bullion delivered to him, and received from him, since the last settlement, as an allowance for necessary waste : *Provided,* That this allowance shall not exceed two-thousandths of the whole amount of gold and silver bullion, respectively, that had been delivered to him by the treasurer.

28. The treasurer shall, from time to time, deliver over to the chief coiner, ingots for the purpose of coinage ; he shall keep a careful record of these transfers, noting the weight and description of the ingots ; and the ingots thus placed in the hands of the chief coiner shall be passed through the several processes necessary to make from them coins, in all respects conformable to law.

29. In adjusting the weights of the coins, the following deviations from the standard weight shall not be exceeded in any of the single pieces—in the dollar and half-dollar, one grain and a half ; in the quarter-dollar, one grain ; in the dime and half-dime, half a grain ; in the gold coins, one-quarter of a grain ;[1] [in the copper coins, one grain in the penny-weight.] And in weighing a large number of pieces together, when delivered from the chief coiner to the treasurer, and from the treasurer to the depositors, the deviations from the standard weight shall

1 See *infra*, 37.

not exceed the following limits—four pennyweights
in one thousand dollars ; three pennyweights in one
thousand half-dollars ; two pennyweights in one
thousand quarter-dollars; one pennyweight in one
thousand dimes ; one pennyweight in one thousand
half-dimes ; two pennyweights in one thousand
eagles; one and a half-pennyweight in one thousand
half-eagles ; one pennyweight in one thousand quarter-eagles.

30. The chief coiner shall, from time to time, as
the coins are prepared, deliver them over to the
treasurer, who shall keep a careful record of their
kind, number and weight ; and, in receiving the
coins, it shall be the duty of the treasurer to see
whether the coins of that delivery are within the
legal limits of the standard weight ; and if his trials
for this purpose shall not prove satisfactory, he shall
cause all the coins of this delivery to be weighed
separately, and such as are not of legal weight shall
be delivered to the melter and refiner, as standard
bullion, to be again formed into ingots and recoined.

31. At every delivery of coins made by the chief
coiner to the treasurer, it shall be the duty of the
treasurer, in the presence of the assayer, to take in-
discriminately, a certain number of pieces of each
variety for the annual trial of coins (the number
being prescribed by the director), which shall be
carefully labeled, and deposited in a chest appropriated for the purpose, kept under the joint care of
the treasurer and assayer, and so secured that neither can have access to its contents without the
presence of the other.

32. The chief coiner shall, from time to time,
deliver to the treasurer the clippings and other por-
tions of bullion remaining after the process of coining ; and the treasurer shall keep a careful record of
their amount.

33. In the treasurer's account with the chief coiner, the chief coiner shall be debited with the amount in weight of standard metal of all the bullion placed in his hands, and credited with the amount, also by weight, of all the coins, clippings and other bullion delivered by him to the treasurer. And once at least in every year, at such time as the director shall appoint, the chief coiner shall deliver to the treasurer all the coins and bullion in his possession, so that his accounts may be settled up to that time ; and, in this settlement, he shall be entitled to a credit for the difference between the whole amount of the ingots delivered to him, and of the coins and bullion received from him, since the last settlement, as an allowance for the necessary waste : *Provided*, That this allowance shall not exceed two-thousandths of the whole amount of the silver, or one and one-half thousandth of the whole amount of the gold, that had been delivered to him by the treasurer.

34. When the coins which are the equivalent to any deposit of bullion are ready for delivery, they shall be paid over to the depositor, or his order, by the treasurer, on a warrant from the director ; and the payment shall be made, if demanded, in the order in which the bullion shall have been brought to the mint, giving priority according to priority of deposit only. And in the denomination of coin delivered, the treasurer shall comply with the wishes of the depositor, unless when impracticable or inconvenient to do so ; in which case the denomination of coin shall be designated by the director.

35. For the purpose of enabling the mint to make returns to depositors with as little delay as possible,[1] it shall be the duty of the secretary of the treasury to keep in the said mint, when the state of the treasury will admit thereof, a deposit of such amount of public money, or of bullion procured for the pur-

See *infra*, 38.

pose, as he shall judge convenient and necessary, not exceeding one million of dollars; out of which those who bring bullion to the mint may be paid the value thereof, as soon as practicable, after this value has been ascertained. The bullion so deposited shall become the property of the United States; no discount or interest shall be charged on moneys so advanced; and the secretary of the treasury may at any time withdraw the said deposit, or any part thereof, or may, at his discretion, allow the coins formed at the mint to be given for their equivalent in other money.

36. To secure a due conformity in the gold and silver coins to their respective standards and weights, an annual trial shall be made of the pieces reserved for this purpose at the mint and its branches, before the judge of the district court of the United States for the eastern district of Pennsylvania, the attorney of the United States for the eastern district of Pennsylvania, and the collector of the port of Philadelphia, and such other persons as the president shall, from time to time, designate for that purpose; who shall meet as commissioners, for the performance of this duty, on the second Monday in February, annually, and may continue their meetings by adjournment, if necessary; and if a majority of the commissioners shall fail to attend at any time appointed for their meeting, then the director of the mint shall call a meeting of the commissioners at such other time as he may deem convenient. And before these commissioners, or a majority of them and in the presence of the officers of the mint, such examination shall be made of the reserved pieces as shall be judged sufficient; and if it shall appear that these pieces do not differ from the standard fineness and weight by a greater quantity than is allowed by law, the trial shall be considered and reported as

satisfactory ; but if any greater deviation from the legal standard or weight shall appear, this fact shall be certified to the president of the United States ; and if, on a view of the circumstances of the case, he shall so decide, the officer or officers implicated in the error shall be thenceforward disqualified from holding their respective offices.

37. In adjusting the weights of gold coins henceforward, the following deviations from the standard weight shall not be exceeded in any of the single pieces—namely, in the double eagle, the eagle and the half-eagle, one-half of a grain, and in the quarter-eagle and gold dollar, one-quarter of a grain. And in weighing a large number of pieces together, when delivered from the chief coiner to the treasurer, and from the treasurer to the depositors, the deviation from the standard weight shall not exceed three pennyweights in one thousand double eagles ; two pennyweights in one thousand eagles ; one and one-half pennyweights in one thousand half-eagles ; one pennyweight in one thousand quarter-eagles ; and one-half of a pennyweight in one thousand gold dollars.—*Act March* 3, 1849.

38. For the purpose of enabling the mint and branch mints of the United States to make returns to depositors with as little delay as possible, it shall be lawful for the president of the United States, when the state of the treasury shall admit thereof, to direct transfers to be made from time to time to the mint and branch mints for such sums of public money as he shall judge convenient and necessary; out of which those who bring bullion to the mint may be paid the value thereof, as soon as practicable after this value has been ascertained. The bullion so deposited shall become the property of the United States ; no discount or interest shall be charged on money so advanced ; and the secretary of the trea-

sury may at any time withdraw the said deposit, or
any part thereof, or may, at his discretion, allow the
coins formed at the mint to be given for their equivalent in other money ; *Provided*, That the bonds
given by the United States treasurers and superintendents of the mint shall be renewed or increased
at the discretion of the secretary of the treasury,
under the operation of this act.—*Act May* 23, 1850.

39. In order to procure bullion for the requisite
coinage of the subdivisions of the dollar authorized
by this act, the treasurer of the mint shall, with the
approval of the director, purchase such bullion with
the bullion fund of the mint. He shall charge himself with the gain arising from the coinage of such
bullion into coins of a nominal value exceeding the
intrinsic value thereof, and shall be credited with
the difference between such intrinsic value and the
price paid for said bullion, and with the expense of
distributing said coins as hereinafter provided. The
balance to his credit, or the profits of said coinage,
shall be, from time to time, on a warrant of the
director of the mint, transferred to the account of
the treasury of the United States.—*Act Feb.* 21, 1853.

40. Such coins shall be paid out at the mint, in
exchange for gold coins at par, in sums not less than
one hundred dollars ; and it shall be lawful, also, to
transmit parcels of the same, from time to time, to
the assistant treasurers, depositaries and other officers of the United States, under general regulations,
proposed by the director of the mint, and approved
by the secretary of the treasury : *Provided, however,*
That the amount coined into quarter-dollars, dimes
and half-dimes, shall be regulated by the secretary
of the treasury.

41. No deposits for coinage into the half-dollar,
quarter-dollar, dime and half-dime, shall hereafter
be received, other than those made by the treasurer

17

of the mint, as herein authorized, and upon account of the United States.

42. At the option of the depositor, gold or silver may be cast into bars or ingots of either pure metal or of standard fineness, as the owner may prefer, with a stamp upon the same, designating its weight and fineness; but no piece, of either gold or silver, shall be cast into bars or ingots of a less weight than ten ounces, except pieces of one ounce, of two ounces, of three ounces and of five ounces, all of which pieces of less weight than ten ounces shall be of the standard fineness, with their weight and fineness stamped upon them. But, in cases, whether the gold and silver deposited be coined or cast into bars or ingots, there shall be a charge to the depositor, in addition to the charge now made for refining or parting the metals, of one-half of one per centum; the money arising from this charge of one-half per centum shall be charged to the treasurer of the mint, and from time to time, on a warrant of the director of the mint, shall be transferred into the treasury of the United States: *Provided, however,* That nothing contained in this section shall be considered as applying to the half-dollar, the quarter-dollar, the dime and half-dime.

43. When gold or silver shall be cast into bars or ingots, or formed into disks at the mint of the United States, or any of the branches thereof, or at any assay office of the United States, the charge for refining, casting or forming said bars, ingots or disks shall be equal to, but not exceed, the actual cost of the operation, including labor, wastage, use of machinery, materials, &c., to be regulated from time to time by the secretary of the treasury.—*Act March* 3, 1853.

44. When private establishments shall be made to refine gold bullion, the secretary of the treasury, if

he shall deem them capable of executing such work, is hereby authorized and required to limit the amount thereof, which shall be refined in the mint at Philadelphia, from quarter to quarter, and to reduce the same progressively as such establishments shall be extended or multiplied ; so as eventually, and as soon as may be, to exclude refining from the mint, and to require that every deposit of gold bullion made therein for coinage shall be adapted to said purpose, without need of refining: *Provided,* That no advances in coin shall be made upon bullion after this regulation shall be carried into effect, except upon bullion refined as herein prescribed.

45. It shall be the duty of the superintendent of the mint to cause to be paid annually into the treasury of the United States the profits of the mint, and to present a quarterly account of the expenditures of the mint to the secretary of the treasury.

*   *   *   *   *   *   *

IV. BRANCHES OF THE MINT.

48. Branches of the mint of the United States shall be established as follows : one branch at the city of New Orleans for the coinage of gold and silver ; one branch at the town of Charlotte, in Mecklinburg county, in the state of North Carolina, for the coinage of gold only ; and one branch at or near Dahlonega, in Lumpkin county, in the state of Georgia, also for the coinage of gold only.—*Act March* 3, 1835.

49. So soon as the necessary buildings are erected for the purpose of well conducting the business of each of the said branches, the following officers[1] shall be appointed upon the nomination of the president, and with the advice and consent of the senate : one superintendent, one treasurer, one assayer, one chief coiner, one melter and one refiner ; and the superintendent of each mint shall engage and employ as many

[1] See *infra,* 53, 55, 57.

clerks and as many subordinate workmen and servants as shall be provided for by law. And the salaries of the said officers and clerks shall be as follows : for the branch at New Orleans, to the superintendent, the sum of two thousand five hundred dollars; to the treasurer, the sum of two thousand dollars; to the chief coiner, the sum of two thousand dollars; to the assayer, melter and refiner, the sum of two thousand dollars each ; to two clerks, the sum of twelve hundred dollars each ;[1] to the subordinate workmen and servants, not exceeding twenty in number, such wages and allowances as are customary and reasonable, according to their respective stations and occupations. For the branches at Charlotte and Dahlonega, to the superintendents, each the sum of two thousand dollars, who shall respectively discharge the duty of treasurers; to the chief coiners, each the sum of one thousand five hundred dollars ; to the assayers, melters and refiners, each the sum of one thousand five hundred dollars ; to the clerks, not exceeding one at each branch, the sum of one thousand dollars ; and to the subordinate workmen and servants, not exceeding the number of five at each of the said branches, such wages and allowances shall be paid as are customary and reasonable, according to their respective stations and occupations.

50. The officers and clerks to be appointed under this act, before entering upon the duties thereof, shall take an oath or affirmation before some judge of the United States, faithfully and diligently to perform the duties thereof; and shall each become bound to the United States of America, with one or more sureties, to the satisfaction of the director of the mint and the secretary of the treasury, with condition for the faithful and diligent performance of the duties of their offices.

[1] See *supra*, 15 ; and *infra*, 65.

51. The general direction of the business of the said branches of the mint of the United States shall be under the control and regulation of the director of the mint at Philadelphia, subject to the approbation of the secretary of the treasury ; and for that purpose, it shall be the duty of the said director to prescribe such regulations, and require such returns periodically, and occasionally, as shall appear to him to be necessary for the purpose of carrying into effect the intention of this act in establishing the said branches; also for the purpose of discriminating the coin which shall be stamped at each branch, and at the mint itself; also for the purpose of preserving uniformity of weight, form and fineness in the coins stamped at each place; and for that purpose, to require the transmission and delivery to him at the mint, from time to time, such parcels of the coinage of each branch as he shall think proper to be subjected to such assays and tests as he shall direct.

52. All the laws and parts of laws made for the regulation of the mint of the United States, and for the government of the officers and persons employed therein, and for the punishment of all offences connected with the mint or coinage of the United States, shall be and the same are hereby declared to be in full force, in relation to each of the branches of the mint by this act established, so far as the same shall be applicable thereto.

53. The officers of the branch mint at New Orleans shall be one superintendent, one treasurer, one assayer, one melter and refiner, and one coiner ; and the officers of the branch mints at Charlotte and Dahlonega severally, shall be one superintendent, who shall also perform the duties of treasurer; one assayer, who shall also perform the duties of melter and refiner; and one coiner. And the annual salaries of the said officers shall be as follows: for the branch

at New Orleans, to the superintendent, two thousand five hundred dollars; to the treasurer, the assayer, the melter and refiner, and the coiner, each two thousand dollars: for the branches at Charlotte and Dahlonega, to the superintendent, two thousand dollars; and to the assayer and the coiner, each fifteen hundred dollars.—*Act Feb.* 13, 1837.

54. That so much of the act entitled "An act to establish branches of the mint of the United States," approved the 3d day of March, 1835, as is inconsistent with the provisions of this act, be and the same is hereby repealed.

55. That an act passed the 13th day of February, 1837, to amend an act entitled "An act to establish branches of the mint of the United States," passed the 3d day of March, 1835, be and it is hereby altered and amended so as to transfer the duties of melter and refiner from the assayer to the coiner at the branches of Dahlonega in Georgia, and of Charlotte in North Carolina, respectively; and that all laws and parts of laws conflicting with this act be and they are hereby repealed.—*Act Feb.* 27, 1843.

56. The oath or affirmation required by the third section of an act passed March 3d, 1835, entitled "An act to establish branches of the mint of the United States," may be taken before any judge of the superior court or of any court of record, in the state where the branch of which the person taking said oath is an officer or clerk, is situated.—*Act April* 2, 1844.

57. That so much of the second section of the act approved March 3d, 1835, entitled "An act to establish branches of the mint of the United States," as vests the appointment of the clerks of the treasurer in the superintendent of each mint, be and the same is hereby repealed; and that the several treasurers of the United States mint be and they are hereby

authorized to appoint their own clerks, subject, however, to the approval of the secretary of the treasury.—*Act March* 3, 1851.

58. That a branch of the mint of the United States
be established in California, to be located by the
secretary of the treasury, for the coinage of gold
and silver.—*Act July* 3, 1852.

59. Suitable buildings shall be procured or erected,
for carrying on the business of said branch mint;
and the following officers shall be appointed, so soon
as the public interests may require their services,
upon the nomination of the president, [by] and with
the advice and consent of the senate, to wit: one
superintendent, one treasurer, one assayer, one melter
and refiner, and one coiner; and the said superintendent shall engage and employ as many clerks,
and as many subordinate workmen and servants, as
shall be provided for by law. And until the 30th of
June, 1855, the salaries of said officers and clerks
shall be as follows: to the superintendent and to the
treasurer, the sum of four thousand five hundred
dollars each; to the assayer, to the melter and refiner, and the coiner, the sum of three thousand
dollars each; to the clerks, the sum of two thousand
dollars each; to the subordinate workmen, such
wages and allowances as are customary and reasonable, according to their respective stations and occupations.

60. The officers and clerks to be appointed under
this act, before entering upon the duties thereof,
shall take an oath or affirmation before some judge
of the United States, or of the supreme court of the
state of California, faithfully and diligently to perform the duties thereof; and shall each become
bound to the United States of America, with one or
more sureties, to the satisfaction of the director of
the mint and the secretary of the treasury, or the
district attorney of the United States for the state

of California, with condition for the faithful and diligent performance of their offices.

61. The general direction of the business of said branch of the mint of the United States shall be under the control and regulation of the director of the mint at Philadelphia, subject to the approbation of the secretary of the treasury ; and, for that purpose, it shall be the duty of the said director to prescribe such regulations, and require such returns periodically and occasionally, as shall appear to him to be necessary for the purpose of carrying into effect the intention of this act in establishing the said branch; also, for the purpose of discriminating the coin which shall be stamped at said branch and at the mint itself; and also for the purpose of preserving uniformity of weight, form and fineness in the coins stamped at said branch ; and for that purpose, to require the transmission and delivery to him at the mint, from time to time, of such parcels of the coinage of said branch as he shall think proper, to be subjected to such assays and tests as he shall direct.

62. That all the laws and parts of laws now in force for the regulation of the mint of the United States, and for the government of the officers and persons employed therein, and for the punishment of all offences connected with the mint or coinage of the United States, shall be and they are hereby declared to be in full force in relation to the branch of the mint by this act established, so far as the same may be applicable thereto.

63. The said branch mint shall be the place of deposit for the public moneys collected in the custom-houses in the state of California, and for such other public moneys as the secretary of the treasury may direct. And the treasurer of said branch mint shall have the custody of the same, and shall perform the duties of an assistant treasurer, and for

that purpose shall be subject to all the provisions contained in an act entitled " An act to provide for the better organization of the treasury, and for the collection, safe-keeping, transfer and disbursement of the public revenue," approved August the 6th, 1846, which relates to the treasurer of the branch mint at New Orleans.

64. If required by the holder, gold in grain or lumps shall be refined, assayed, cast into bars or ingots, and stamped in said branch mint, or in the mint of the United States, or any of its branches, in such manner as may indicate the value and fineness of the bar or ingot; which shall be paid for by the owner or holder of said bullion, at such rates and charges, and under such regulations, as the director of the mint, under the control of the secretary of the treasury, may from time to time establish.

65. That the seventh section of the act of 18th January, 1837, entitled " An act supplementary to an act establishing the mint, and regulating the coins of the United States," be so amended as to extend the allowance for the annual salary of the clerks in the branch mint of the United States at New Orleans, to eighteen hundred dollars each, from and after the first day of July, 1854, at the discretion of the officers authorized by law to appoint, with the approbation of the President of the United States.—*Act March* 3, 1855.

V. ASSAY OFFICE.

66. The secretary of the treasury is hereby authorized and required to establish in the city of New York an office for the receipt, and for the melting, refining, parting and assaying of gold and silver bullion and foreign coin, and for casting the same into bars, ingots or disks. The assistant treasurer of the United States in New York shall be treasurer

18

of the said assay office; and the secretary of the
treasury shall, with the approbation and consent of
the president of the United States, appoint such
other officers and clerks, authorize the employment
of such assistants, workmen and servants as shall be
necessary for the proper conduct and management
of the said office and of the business pertaining
thereto, at such compensation as shall be approved
by the president : *Provided*, That the same shall not
exceed that allowed for corresponding services under existing laws relating to the mint of the United
States and its branches.—*Act March* 3, 1853.

67. The owner or owners of any gold or silver
bullion, in dust or otherwise, or of any foreign coin,
shall be entitled to deposit the same in the said office, and the treasurer thereof shall give a receipt,
stating the weight and description thereof, in the
manner and under the regulations that are or may
be provided in like cases or deposits at the mint of
the United States with the treasurer thereof. And
such bullion shall, without delay, be melted, parted,
refined and assayed, and the net value thereof, and
of all foreign coins deposited in said office, shall be
ascertained; and the treasurer shall thereupon forth-
with issue his certificate of the net value thereof,
payable in coins of the same metal as that deposited,
either at the office of the assistant treasurer of the
United States, in New York, or at the mint of the
United States, at the option of the depositor, to be
expressed in the certificate ; which certificates shall
be receivable at any time, within sixty days from
the date thereof, in payment of all debts due to the
United States at the port of New York, for the full
sum therein certified. All gold or silver bullion and
foreign coin deposited, melted, parted, refined or
assayed as aforesaid, shall, at the option of the depositor, be cast in the said office into bars, ingots or

disks, either of pure metal or of standard fineness (as the owner may prefer), with a stamp thereon of such form and device as shall be prescribed by the secretary of the treasury, accurately designating its weight and fineness : *Provided,* That no ingot, bar or disk shall be cast of less weight than five ounces, unless the same be of standard fineness, and of either one, two or three ounces in weight. And all gold or silver bullion and foreign coin intended by the depositor to be converted into coins of the United States, shall, as soon as assayed and its net value certified as above provided, be transferred to the mint of the United States, under such directions as shall be made by the secretary of the treasury, and at the expense of the contingent fund of the mint, and shall there be coined. And the secretary of the treasury is hereby authorized, with the approval of the president of the United States, to make the necessary regulations for the adjustment of the accounts between the respective officers, upon the transfer of any bullion or coin between the assay office, the mint, and assistant treasurer in New York.

68. The operations of melting, parting, refining and assaying in the said office shall be under the general directions of the director of the mint, in subordination to the secretary of the treasury ; and it shall be the duty of the said director to prescribe such regulations, and to order such tests, as shall be requisite to insure faithfulness, accuracy and uniformity in the operations of the said office.

69. The laws of the United States for the government of the mint and its officers in relation to the receipt, payment, custody of deposits and settlement of accounts, the duties and responsibilities of officers and others employed therein, the oath to be taken and the bonds and sureties to be given by them (as

far as the same may be applicable), shall extend to the assay office hereby established, to its officers, assistants, clerks, workmen and others employed therein.

70. The same charges shall be made and demanded at the said assay office for refining, parting, casting into bars, ingots or disks, and for alloy, as are or shall be made and demanded at the mint ; and no other charges shall be made to depositors than by law are authorized to be made at the mint. And the amount received from the charges hereby authorized shall be accounted for and appropriated for defraying the contingent expenses of the said office.

71. The secretary of the treasury is authorized to procure, by rent, lease or otherwise, a building or apartments in the city of New York, suitable for the operations of said office, unless he shall be of opinion that suitable apartments in the custom-house in that city may be assigned for this purpose. And he is also hereby authorized and directed to procure the necessary machinery and implements for the carrying on the operations and business of the said office.

Laws Relating to Coinage.

COINS OF THE UNITED STATES.

1. There shall be from time to time struck and coined at the said mint, coins of gold, silver and copper, of the following denominations, values and descriptions, viz. : eagles—each to be of the value of ten dollars or units, [and to contain two hundred and forty-seven grains and four-eighths of a grain of pure, or two hundred and seventy grains of standard gold.] Half-eagles—each to be of the value of five dollars,

[and to contain one hundred and twenty-three grains and six-eighths of a grain of pure, or one hundred and thirty-five grains of standard gold.] Quarter-eagles—each to be of the value of two dollars and a half-dollar, [and to contain sixty-one grains and seven-eighths of a grain of pure, or sixty-seven grains and four-eighths of a grain of standard gold.] Dollars or units—each to be of the value of a Spanish milled dollar as the same is now current, [and to contain three hundred and seventy-one grains and four-sixteenth parts of a grain of pure, or four hundred and sixteen grains of standard silver.] Half-dollars—each to be of half the value of the dollar or unit, [and to contain one hundred and eighty-five grains and ten-sixteenth parts of a grain of pure, or two hundred and eight grains of standard silver.] Quarter-dollars—each to be of one-fourth the value of the dollar or unit, [and to contain ninety-two grains and thirteen-sixteenth parts of a grain of pure, or one hundred and four grains of standard silver.] Dismes—each to be of the value of one-tenth of a dollar or unit, [and to contain thirty-seven grains and two-sixteenth parts of a grain of pure, or forty-one grains and three-fifth parts of a grain of standard silver.] Half-dismes—each to be of the value of one-twentieth of a dollar, [and to contain eighteen grains and nine-sixteenth parts of a grain of pure, or twenty grains and four-fifth parts of a grain of standard silver.] Cents—each to be of the value of one-hundredth part of a dollar, [and to contain eleven pennyweights of copper. Half-cents—each to be of the value of half a cent, and to contain five pennyweights and half a pennyweight of copper.][1]—*Act April* 2, 1792.

2. The proportional value of gold to silver in all coins which shall by law be current as money within

[1] The contents of the several coins have been altered by subsequent laws ; see *infra,* 4, 5, 13, 17.

the United States, shall be as fifteen to one, according to quantity in weight of pure gold or pure silver;
that is to say, every fifteen pounds weight of pure
silver shall be of equal value in all payments, with
one pound weight of pure gold, and so in proportion
as to any greater or less quantities of the respective
metals.

3. The standard for both gold and silver coins of
the United States shall hereafter be such, that of one
thousand parts by weight, nine hundred shall be of
pure metal, and one hundred of alloy ; and the alloy
of the silver coins shal be of copper ; and the alloy
of the gold coins shall be of copper and silver, provided that the silver do not exceed one-half of the
whole alloy.—*Act Jan.* 18, 1837.

4. Of the silver coins, the dollar shall be of the
weight of four hundred and twelve and one-half
grains ; [the half-dollar of the weight of two hundred
and six and one-fourth grains; the quarter-dollar of
the weight of one hundred and three and one-eighth
grains ; the dime, or tenth part of a dollar, of the
weight of forty-one and a quarter grains ; and the
half-dime, or twentieth part of a dollar, of the weight
of twenty grains, and five-eighths of a grain.[1] And
that dollars, half-dollars and quarter dollars, dimes and
half-dimes, shall be legal tenders of payment, according to their nominal value, for any sums whatever.

5. Of the gold coins, the weight of the eagle shall
be two hundred and fifty-eight grains ; that of the
half-eagle one hundred and twenty-nine grains ; and
that of the quarter-eagle sixty-four and one-half
grains. And that for all sums whatever, the eagle
shall be a legal tender of payment for ten dollars ;
the half-eagle for five dollars ; and the quarter-eagle
for two and a half dollars.

6. The silver coins heretofore issued at the mint

[1] Altered—*infra*, 13.

of the United States, and the gold coins issued since the 31st day of July, 1834, shall continue to be legal tenders of payment for their nominal values, on the same terms as if they were of the coinage provided for by this act.

7. Upon the coins struck at the mint there shall be the following devices and legends : upon one side of each of said coins there shall be an impression emblematic of liberty, with an inscription of the word LIBERTY, and the year of the coinage ; and upon the reverse of each of the gold and silver coins, there shall be the figure or representation of an eagle, with the inscription United States of America, and a designation of the value of the coin ; but on the reverse of the dime and half-dime, cent [and half-cent] the figure of the eagle shall be omitted.

8. There shall be, from time to time, struck and coined at the mint of the United States, and the branches thereof, conformably in all respects to law, (except that on the reverse of the gold dollar the figure of the eagle shall be omitted), and conformably in all respects to the standard for gold coins now established by law, coins of gold of the following denominations and value, viz. : double eagles, each to be of the value of twenty dollars, or units, and gold dollars, each to be of the value of one dollar, or unit.—*Act March* 3, 1849.

9. For all sums whatever, the double eagle shall be a legal tender for twenty dollars, and the gold dollar shall be a legal tender for one dollar.

10. All laws now in force in relation to the coins of the United States, and the striking and coining the same, shall, so far as applicable, have full force and effect in relation to the coins herein authorized, whether the said laws are penal or otherwise ; and whether they are for preventing counterfeiting or debasement, for protecting the currency, for regulat-

ing and guarding the process of striking and coining,
and the preparations therefor, or for the security of
the coin, or for any other purpose.

11. In adjusting the weights of gold coins henceforward, the following deviations from the standard
weight shall not be exceeded in any of the single
pieces—namely, in the double eagle, the eagle, and
the half-eagle, one-half of a grain, and in the quarter-
eagle, and gold dollar, one-quarter of a grain ; and
that, in weighing a large number of pieces together,
when delivered from the chief coiner to the treasurer,
and from the treasurer to the depositors, the deviation
from the standard weight shall not exceed three
pennyweights in one thousand double eagles ; two
pennyweights in one thousand eagles ; and and one-
half pennyweights in one thousand half-eagles ; one
pennyweight in one thousand quarter-eagles; and one-
half of a pennyweight in one thousand gold dollars.

12. It shall be lawful to coin at the mint of the
United States and its branches, a piece of the denomination and legal value of three cents, or three-
hundredths of a dollar, to be composed of three-
fourths silver and one-fourth copper, and to weigh
twelve grains and three-eighths of a grain ;[1] that the
said coin shall bear such devices as shall be conspicuously different from those of the other silver
coins, and of the gold dollar, but having the inscription United States of America, and its denomination
and date ; and that it shall be a legal tender in payment of debts for all sums of thirty cents and under.
And that no ingots shall be used for the coinage of
the three cent pieces herein authorized, of which the
quality differs more than five-thousandths from the
legal standard ; and that, in adjusting the weight of
the said coin, the following deviations from the
standard weight shall not be exceeded, namely,
one-half of a grain in the single piece, and one

1 Altered—*infra*, 16.

pennyweight in a thousand pieces.—*Act March* 3, 1851.

13. The weight of the half-dollar or piece of fifty cents shall be one hundred and ninety-two grains, and the quarter-dollar, dime, and half-dime, shall be, respectively, one-half, one-fifth, and one-tenth of the weight of said half-dollar.—*Act Feb.* 21, 1853.

14. The silver coins issued in conformity with the above section, shall be legal tenders in payment of debts for all sums not exceeding five dollars.

15. From time to time there shall be struck and coined at the mint of the United States, and the branches thereof, conformably in all respects to law, and conformably in all respects to the standard of gold coins now established by law, a coin of gold of the value of three dollars, or units, and all the provisions of an act entitled "An act to authorize the coinage of gold dollars and double eagles," approved March 3d, 1849, shall be applied to the coin herein authorized, so far as the same may be applicable, but the devices and shape of the three dollar piece shall be fixed by the secretary of the treasury.

16. And the secretary of the treasury is hereby authorized to regulate the size and the devices of the new silver coin, authorized by an act entitled "An act amendatory of existing laws relative to the half-dollar, quarter-dollar, dime and half-dime," passed at the present session; and that, to procure such devices, as also the models, moulds and matrices or original dies for the coins, disks or ingots authorized by said act, the director of the mint is empowered, with the approval of the secretary of the treasury, to engage temporarily for that purpose the services of one or more artists, distinguished in their respective departments, who shall be paid for such services from the contingent appropriation for the mint : And that hereafter the three cent coin now

19

authorized by law shall be made of the weight of three-fiftieths of the weight of the half-dollar, as provided in said act, and of the same standard of fineness. And the said act entitled "An act amendatory of existing laws relative to the half-dollar, quarter-dollar, dime, and half-dime," shall take effect and be in full force from and after the 1st day of April, 1853, anything therein to the contrary notwithstanding.—*Act March* 3, 1853.

17. The standard weight of the cent coined at the mint shall be seventy-two grains, or three-twentieths of one ounce troy, with no greater deviation than four grains in each piece ; and said cent shall be composed of eighty-eight per centum of copper and twelve per centum of nickel, of such shape and device as may be fixed by the director of the mint, with the approbation of the secretary of the treasury ; and the coinage of the half-cent shall cease.—*Act Feb.* 21, 1857.

18. The treasurer of the mint, under the instruction of the secretary of the treasury, shall from time to time, purchase from the bullion fund of the mint the materials necessary for the coinage of such cent piece, and transfer the same to the proper operative officers of the mint to be manufactured and returned in coin. And the laws in force relating to the mint and the coinage of the precious metals, and in regard to the sale and distribution of the copper coins, shall, so far as applicable, be extended to the coinage herein provided for : *Provided,* That the nett profits of said coinage, ascertained in like manner as is prescribed in the second section of this act, shall be transferred to the treasury of the United States.

19. It shall be lawful to pay out the said cent at the mint in exchange for any of the gold and silver coins of the United States, and also in exchange for the former copper coins issued : and it shall be law-

ful to transmit parcels of the said cents, from time
to time, to the assistant treasurers, depositaries and
other officers of the United States, under general
regulations proposed by the director of the mint,
and approved by the secretary of the treasury, for
exchange as aforesaid. And it shall also be lawful
for the space of two years from the passage of this
act and no longer, to pay out at the mint the cents
aforesaid for the fractional parts of the dollar here-
inbefore named, at their nominal value of twenty-
five, twelve-and-half and six-and-quarter cents, respectively.

LIST OF DIRECTORS OF THE MINT, FROM ITS ORGANIZATION TO THE YEAR 1858.

David Rittenhouse (the eminent philosopher), July, 1792 to July, 1795.

Henry William De Saussure (vice Mr. Rittenhouse resigned), July 11th, to Oct. 28, 1795, (afterwards and for many years Chancellor of South Carolina).

Elias Boudinot (in place of Judge De Saussure resigned), October, 1795, to July, 1805. (Previously President of Congress under the confederation).

Robert Patterson (on the resignation of Dr. Boudinot), July, 1805, to July, 1824. (Vice Provost of the University of Pennsylvania, and President American Philosophical Society.

Dr. Samuel Moore (in place of Mr. Patterson deceased), July, 1824, to July, 1835. (Member of Congress from Bucks county, Pa.)

Dr. Robert M. Patterson (on the resignation of Dr. Moore), July, 1835, to July, 1851. (Professor of Natural Philosophy in University, Virginia, and President of American Philosophical Society).

Dr. Geo. N. Eckert (vice Dr. Patterson resigned), July, 1851, to April, 1853. (Member of Congress from Lebanon county, Pa.)

Thos. M. Pettit (in place of Dr. Eckert resigned), April to June, 1853. (Judge District Court, Philadelphia).

The present incumbent, James Ross Snowden, (previously Speaker of the House of Representatives, Pennsylvania, Treasurer of Pennsylvania, and Treasurer of the Mint), was appointed in June, 1853, in the place of Judge Pettit, who died on the 31st of May, in that year, having held the office of Director but a few weeks.

SUPPLEMENT No. 1.

N E. shillings and sixpences, $20 to $25.

Pine tree shilling, about $5.   Sixpence, 3 pence and 2 pence, more.

Baltimore shilling, sixpence and groat, $31.

Chalmers' Annapolis shilling—poor, $5.

Carolina Elephant piece, bored, $10.

Rosa Americana, set, $10.

Washington cents, 1791 and 1792, from $6 to $10.

Virginia piece, about $2.

Early dollars and halves, average $3 each.

Flying eagle, dollars and halves, 1836, '38 and '39, $5 and $10 each, and even more.

Dollars of 1804, 1851, 1852, each $5.

Gold dollar 1836, $7; 1852, $10.

Dimes and halves prior to 1815, about $1 each,

Cent of 1779, $5; 1793, $1·50 to $2.   Pattern cent 1854, $1·50.

Half cent 1831, $10 ; 1836, $5.

SUPPLEMENT No. 2.

Statement of the amount of coinage executed at the mint of the United States and its branches in No. of pieces, during the years 1856 and '57.

Denomination.	1856.	1857.
GOLD :		
Double Eagles,...............	1,513,878	1,439,875
Eagles,......................	148,490	48,106
Half-Eagles,.................	350,333	246,594
Three-Dollars, ...	60,510	34,891
Quarter-Eagles, ...	485,247	318,494
Dollars, ...	1,788,996	801,602
Fine bars,...................	4,937	7,316
Unparted bars,..............	928	
SILVER :		
Dollars, ...	63,500	94,000
Half-Dollars,............... .	3,807,000	2,964,000
Quarter-Dollars, ...	8,518,000	10,906,000
Dimes, ...	6,960,000	7,120,000
Half-Dimes, ...	5,980,000	8,660,000
Three-Cent pieces,...........	1,458,000	1,042,000
Fine bars,...................	254	840
COPPER :		
Cents, ...	2,690,463	17,833,456
Half-Cents,.................	40,430	35,180
RECAPITULATION :		
Total pieces coined,..........	33,870,966	51,552,354
Total value,................	$64,567,142·30	$60,532,365·91

INDEX.

Plate 1

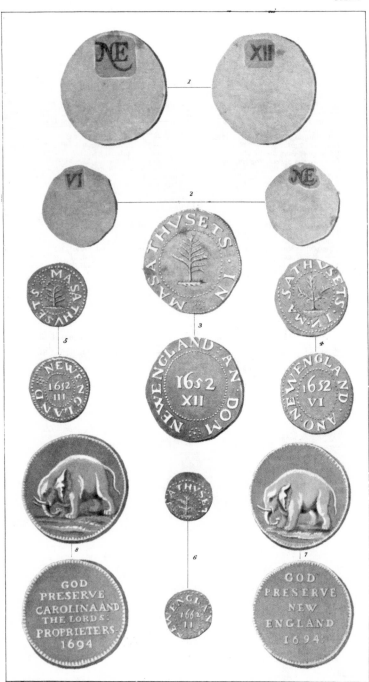

Plate 2

Plate 3

— 1 —

— 2 —

— 3 —

— 4 —

— 5 —

Engraved & Printed by J.E. Gavit.

Albany.

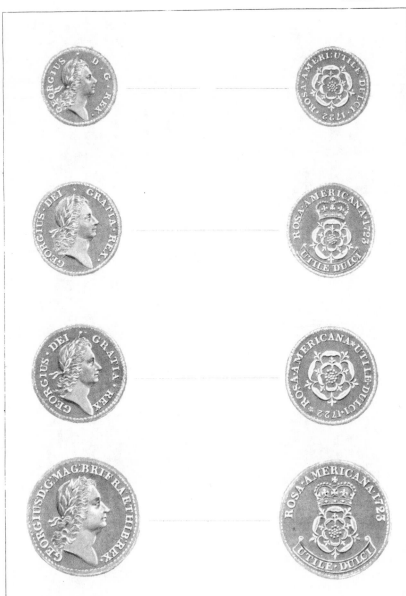

Engraved & Printed by J.E. Gavit